Rained Off

RAINED OFF

A STORY ABOUT HARDWORKING MEN

by Paddy Byrne

First published in 2011
by Roger Byrne
14 Mount Stuart Square
Cardiff Bay, South Wales CF10 5DP

British Library Cataloguing in Publication Data
A CIP catalogue record for this book is available from the British Library

ISBN 978-0-9570239-0-1

Book design by Jamie Kerry for Belle Étoile Studios
www.belleetoilestudios.com

Printed and bound in Great Britain

Thank you to Paddy Byrne for being our dad.

*Roger Byrne would like to thank Patricia Prizeman,
Sara Malone, Michael Trudeau, and Jamie Kerry
for their help in getting this book edited, designed,
and printed to such a high standard.*

Foreword

I am Roger Anthony Byrne, the youngest son of Paddy Byrne. I was born in London in 1960. My brothers and sisters are, from oldest to youngest, Don, Bill, Pat, Maureen, Frances, Robert, Ian, Fiona, and Sean, and then there's myself.

I hope you enjoy reading my father's book and that it makes you smile many times, as this was his wish.

Patrick Byrne (he had no middle name) was born in Gweedore, County Donegal, Ireland, on 21 July 1926. He had two sisters, Fanny (the eldest of the family) and Annie (the youngest), and two brothers, Briney (Bernard), who was older, and Sean (pronounced Shan), who was younger. There were also Rodger, Sarah, Denis, and Dan, all of whom died at very young ages.

They have all now passed away, my father being the last to die, on 2 August 2010 at the age of eighty-four, in Charing Cross Hospital, Hammersmith, London, from a bleeding peptic ulcer, which led to pneumonia.

His brothers and sisters made their way over to Glasgow to find work prior to the outbreak of the Second World War, and my father ventured over during the war. Briney and Fanny settled in Glasgow and stayed there, whilst Sean settled in Perth, Scotland, and Annie stayed in Annagry, Loughanure, Donegal, with their father John Ruari, as their mother Bridget had died in 1933 at the age of thirty-six, after having nine children.

My father met my mother Laura Rankin, who was from Inverness, Scotland, and they were married 31 December 1944. They lived in Perth before going over to live in Donegal for a while, and they finally settled in London in 1957.

This book was written by my father over the course of a year or so. In it he remembers episodes of his life on the construction sites and in the tunnels throughout the United Kingdom, including the Victoria line on the London Underground in 1962–1964 and the original Channel Tunnel that was abandoned in 1974–1975. He was no Flann O'Brien or James Joyce to the writing world, but he wrote with his own honest style. He learnt much about writing from his oldest brother Briney, in Glasgow.

Briney, under his official name of Bernard J. Byrne, wrote many poems, stories, and recitals, much of them in Gaelic. He also wrote a book titled *The Strumpet of Glenaree*, published by Rossan Sweeney Publishing. Briney died in January 2000.

You will find these stories honest and amusing and hopefully be able to transport your imagination to the very building site canteen or local pub where each chapter and story is told at the time. Try to be amongst the men as they drank, swapped stories, and looked out the window at the weather, whilst putting all their own personal problems and family worries to one side. At times you will notice the grammar in this book is not strictly the Queen's English, but it captures how many of the characters spoke at the time.

It is imperative for our generation not to lose touch with the likes of these hardworking men, from a bygone era. This book is a down-to-earth example of such men's workdays from 1945 to the 1960s, and you can feel the toil, poverty, and rough surroundings they and their families endured. Historians will love it.

My mother is still alive and remains in the little council flat in Hammersmith, London, that she shared with my father before he died. They were married for sixty-five years.

Unfortunately most of the characters in this book have now passed on and are laid with dignity in the very earth they toiled over the harsh years of their lives. The names have been changed out of respect for privacy, but I did get to meet many of the men throughout my teenage years, around Shepherd's Bush, London; Glasgow; Annagry, Donegal; and when I started out in the construction industry as a bricklayer in 1977.

They were the most honourable rogues you could ever meet. Respect to the "Donegal Tunnel Tigers".

—*Roger A. Byrne*
August 2011

Acknowledgements

Speaking on behalf of my brothers, sisters, and our mother, we'd like to thank *all* of our many relatives in Ireland and Scotland.

A special thanks to everyone in Annagry, Loughanure, Donegal. I know Paddy would want to give a special mention to his mother, father, brothers, sisters, their children, and everyone in Sharkey's Bar, where he felt most at home.

Thanks also to everyone who worked alongside our father, on the building sites, in the tunnels, and especially in the pubs—not forgetting the publicans, who enjoyed the stories firsthand.

I was told the following by a great publican Mr Michael Conway, who owned many pubs around West London and Ireland and was a very close friend of my father: "Paddy told me the same stories one hundred times, and one hundred times I laughed."

Thank you, Paddy Byrne.

Paddy Byrne in 1951 walking in Perth High Street, Scotland

Chapter 1

The winter of fifty-nine was indeed a winter of discontent, if not a winter of rain. It was for me anyway, regardless of what the statisticians might say. Perhaps my travelling throughout the country placed me in the wettest places at the wettest times, though it started out in London, and London is not considered a rainforest area, like Manchester for instance.

I was working on the site of a new post office sorting centre in Newman Street, off Oxford Street in the West End of London, when the rain came, and like the monsoons, it stayed. Starting foul one November morning, a real winter morning, and a Monday morning to boot. What more could you ask for.

That morning as I was approaching the site entrance I was overhauled by a working colleague named of McDaid, who nodded in greeting. It was futile to say anything, for the wind and rain would blow the words away. Like myself he was bent against the storm, chin on chest, with his hands gripping hard to keep his old buttonless donkey jacket tight about himself. McDaid wore no cap, and his hair was plastered to his forehead. His shirt was open to the waist under the donkey jacket. He was of the younger generation, and as hard as iron. They tore around the place as if the devil himself was after them. A complete contrast to me and my ilk, who plodded on at a steady gait, just like the old plough horse.

As we turned into the site entrance under the lee of the huge doors, we got a reprieve, and our faces glowed red in thanksgiving. Here we paused awhile to get our breath back, and to shake the wet from our sodden clothes.

Old Jock the site checker was observing us from the porch of his gate-house. He was in the warm and dry, for he wore no jacket, just an old brown cardigan which was his garb winter or summer.

"Bad morning boys," he coughed, as he thumped his hollow-sounding chest. He was forever complaining about his chest, and striking it as he did so, thus earning himself the nickname "Mea Culpa".

"Fuck all wrong with it," growled McDaid, as he shook the rain from his jacket, sending a spray of water towards Jock.

I glanced sideways at him, two bloodshot eyes told their own story.

"Old Mea Culpa don't like the damp weather," he added, nodding to-wards Jock's back, who was now disappearing into the gloom of his bower. "He never stops moaning and groaning while thumping that chest of his. No bloody wonder he has a hump on his back, that chest of his has been pile-driven back there over the years as he creeps about like a mouse with the whooping cough."

"Aye," I said. "I must admit he is a bit dowdy by times, right enough." I shook the rain from my bonnet.

"There won't be anything doing today Pat, it is on for the day," said McDaid, as he looked around the wet and desolated site. "Anyway I'm off to the toilets, as I've got two bottles of beer here, thank God for yon owld boy in the off-sales, he is a decent owld bugger, for he is not suppose to sell it until half past ten. Do you want one?"

"No, no. Not at this time of the morning, but thanks. I'll see you later."

He made off at a gallop towards the wash house, while I braced my shoulder against the storm, and headed for the site canteen.

The canteen was a long timber building standing in a corner of the site, and contained nothing more exciting than a few military-type tables, with a variety of chairs and stools and a serving hatch from the kitchen. Oh yes!—there was an old poster on the wall, telling you not to stand on nails.

On entering, I found most of the occupants engrossed in their news-papers. Football, and horseracing pages getting the main attention. Sure there was nothing else happening in their world worthy of the same scrutiny. Slugging tea from large mugs was done automatically. Later on, should the adverse weather continue, a few packs of cards would materi-alise.

Nap, Crib, and Pontoon were the most common games played. Of course some of the Irish contingent would go for their national game of twenty-five. The game was as complicated as themselves. It took many years of practice before you dared sit into a school of play, for stakes. Most building workers could play with confidence. I never could. Of course the Irish were in their element here, having learned the game as boys back in their own country, where thick ears emphasised, and corrected any leaning toward error.

On my entry, there was just one game in progress. A game of crib between four steel fixers seated behind the door. One of them was also engaged in slagging a fellow workmate at an adjacent table, while he dealt the cards. Something to do with his inability to carry his drink during the weekend. Things were indeed normal for a Monday morning.

I made for my usual table, where the timber men sat. This was situated at the far end of the canteen, next to the service hatch. Being so placed made it unsuitable for the card players, as the busy hatch spoiled their concentration. It suited us fine.

There were six of us timber men on site. Our job was the shoring up of surrounding buildings, bracing them and underpinning their foundations where necessary, also the timbering of any deep excavation taking place on site.

Building-site personnel are made up of numerous small gangs each carrying out their own functions under the supervision of a gangerman or foreman, whatever the case may be. They in turn are answerable to the section foreman, or "walking pelter" as nicknamed. All are under the command of the general foreman, or "GF" as he was referred to.

Gangs are inclined to stick together, be it in canteen or pub, and rib each other rotten. The black gang—machine drivers and fitters—was the odd one out. They were left very much on their own. An attitude something akin to that of a ship's crew. Engine room and deck. Of course when they met off site or "off hire"* things were different—that is, providing there were none of their own ilk around.

"Morning boys," I said, taking the space offered to me on the end of a stool. The occupant having moved along.

---

* unemployed

"Morning … Wet … You're late," a grunt came in turns from around the table. The grunt came from behind a large newspaper.

"No work today Pat?" said Tom Tinen, seated opposite me. Tom was also my working partner, as we worked in pairs. He always wore his cap with the stud open. Why, I'll never know. It was the first thing he did when he bought a new one. A small broad-set man in his fifties, and hailed from County Tipperary. A place he hadn't seen since he was seventeen.

"I knew it last night when this old shoulder of mine started playing up," he continued, rubbing his left shoulder. "It always seems to know when rain is in the offing, tis strange how it affects the bones."

"I'm thinking it affects more than the bones," scowled Ginger Freel. "That is, if the behaviour of yon new gangerman is anything to go by. He was out there earlier on, roaring his head off, shaking his fist in the air, while dog dancing in a puddle of water. He reminded you of one of them black protestors on the march."

"What was annoying him?" I asked.

"Don't rightly know," said Tinen. "Probably the rain is stopping him from making a name for himself seeing as he is new around here. Though I did hear someone say that he wanted some cement moved around in the cement shed, and his gang refused to do it, maintaining that as everybody else were rained off, so were they, quite right too. Fuck the old clouster."

A murmur of agreement went round the table.

"Cup of tay Pat?" asked Ginger, as he rose and made for the hatch.

I nodded. Ginger was a nice bloke. A Mayo man, he was settled down locally, having given up the tramping some years before, when he was about thirty. Perhaps there was a woman behind it. He returned with the tea.

"I met old Mickey Duffy on the bus this morning," continued Ginger, as he used his finger to chase a floating tea leaf around in his mug. "Him being in that old clouster's gang, I asked him what was he like. Now you know Mickey and his ways. He just lifted his cap, and scratched yon old head of his before answering. 'Well,' said he, 'sure now he is like the hen on the half door, you don't know whether she is going to shite inside or outside.'"

That brought a laugh.

Most of the men on site were of the younger generation, with that generation's ways. Good men though, otherwise they would not be there. The rest were of the old school, and stretched in years from forty to sixty, more so the timber men. Most of them had tramped the country over, in the bad old days. I doubt if you could mention a major contract that took place over the last forty years between John o' Groats and Lands End but someone present had worked on it.

Some of them were married but still on the move. Others were, but had parted company somewhere along the line. Of course some were just passing through—the tramp navvy, or "long-distance men", as they were called. They never stayed long anywhere, and generally dossed down in some lodging house or kip, during their stay. Those men walked the roads, never by public transport, as they maintained you could pass good work doing so. They took an odd lift of course, when offered, and that was often or not given by some builder's lorry, delivering to a site. In fact they were the only lorries they would thumb, knowing there was bound to be work where it was heading. They were usually set to work no matter where they went, being the best of workmen. They also had all the news from various contracts up and down the country, and their crack was good. Good men to have around too, for they often had the answer for many tricky problems that can arise on site. They had seen it all before.

Among their ranks, of English, Irish, Scots, and Welsh, could be found the occasional boffin too, highly educated, and of an unknown background. The navvies have but the one nationality. The one religion, and the one hard slog.

"Do you know something," said Big Bill Magehie, as he placed his paper on the table, and began to roll a cigarette. Bill was a Geordie, with a heavy Tyneside accent. "Them papers you get nowadays are worth nought, just a load of rubbish." He frowned as he looked over his shoulder towards a commotion taking place among the tables behind us.

"Them card clowns are getting ready to start! That's the end of peace and quiet now, especially when them twenty-five mobsters start knocking the table."

"Fluke off!" came the roar from somewhere behind. Some non-player was getting the heave-ho to make room for a fellow player. "If you were as enthusiastic about work as you are about fluking cards, there wouldn't be a site in the country big enough for you. Ye parcel of twats."

"Ach, awa an piss in a tin," came the Scottish reply.

"All we need now is some bugger to make a bloomer at the twenty-five table, and the ceilidh will be truly on its way," said young Bob Lynch, who sat at our neighbouring table. At twenty, he was the youngest man on site.

"There must be a few shillings still left in the kitty after the weekend," somebody muttered.

"I see here," said Bill Magehie, changing the subject as he picked up his paper again. "A man in Glasgow has been given thirty days, for abusing a cat, a bit stiff for that offence."

"Must have been bad abuse for sure," said Ginger, as he spun his empty mug in a circle with his finger. "But talking about cats, I once knew a man up in a place called Blairgowrie, in Scotland, who used to cut cats as a sideline. Five bob a time. Well you know what I mean by cutting. Dressing, in spinster's language. He used to do it with his tobacco knife, reckoning that tobacco was a great steriliser. The old bugger."

"Must have had a hell o' a job holding them," said Bill, placing his paper back on the table, and throwing away his stub of a cigarette, to bring forth his pipe. "A tomcat is not easy to hold at the best o' times, never mind when one is trying to cut the stones out of him at the same time. How the hell did he do it?"

"Oh he maintained it was dead-easy like. You see, he took one arm out of his jacket then with the other hand still in the jacket, he grabbed tom by the scruff of the neck, and yanked him halfways up that sleeve as it turned inside out. Now all that was visible of puss were his hindquarters. So he went about his business at his leisure. When finished, he just yanked him out by the hind legs, and dropped him, that is if you could now call him a him! Needless to say the cat made off like a bat out o' hell. Mind you he moaned that the operation was sore on the lining of his sleeves."

"Holy hell!" exclaimed Bill. "He should have been hung for that."

"Cripes I'm no lover of cats," I said, "but that was rough. No bloody wonder the moggie scarpered, but hadn't he left it a bit late though. Not much sense in scooting off when the best part of him was left on the deck.

"This man in Glasgow was a saint by comparison," said Ginger. "Apparently he had fallen out with the woman in the flat below, so to annoy her, or perhaps to get even with her, he stuck four seashells on his cat's paws, and let him loose about the floor. Now if I know anything about the part of Glasgow he came from, wax cloth would be the only covering on that floor. That is, if there were anything atall. So you can well imagine the clatter made by the cat as he galloped about. No doubt he gave him a spool or something to play with, just to keep him on the move. It must have got to her right enough, for she sent for the police, telling them that the man upstairs was keeping a Clydesdale horse in the house without cooperation's approval. That's how they found the shod cat."

"By dad," I said. "He must have annoyed her truly, for her to send for the police, a thing they don't do lightly up there. I remember once when staying in the Model Lodging House in Portugal Street, Glasgow, an old boy stopping there, always swore there were three people you should never let darken your door. A policeman, a doctor, or a priest, that was his philosophy."

"I once knew a Pole," whispered Mick Ryan. His nickname was "Whispering Mick". "We worked together on a hydro rock tunnel job. He told me how they done away with cats back in his country. They put their neck in the door jam, and then slammed the door. Bang! Just like hanging, it broke the neck right away."

"I suppose when you think of it, it was no more cruel than hanging or garrotting," said Ginger.

"Talking about cats," chimed in Young Bob. "Back in my county they drown them, by tying them up in a bag with a big stone for company, but they have a far better time of it than the dog. There was this man near us who used to sweep the chimney with the dog. On my oath he did! He would go up on the roof with a length of rope, which he dropped down the chimney to the wife who was waiting below with the dog. She tied the rope round the dog's waist, and then gave it a tug. That was the signal for him to start hauling up. Mind you them old chimneys were very wide. It was said that he used to break into that song 'Haul away Joe' while doing so, but I never heard him. He always made out that the dog didn't mind atall, as long as the fire was out, and seeing as he enjoyed a good feed of spuds afterwards. For dessert, he got slung in the lake. My father said he didn't doubt but the dog took it all in his stride, seeing he was so seldom fed, and it explained why he was forever perched in front of the fire looking up the chimney, he was looking for soot.""Ach, bugger off," said Jim Carney, as he made a swing at the young fellow with his cap. "Indeed I wouldn't put it past them down where you come from."

"Be japers! Going about castrating cats at five bob a time was a lucrative crack," said Tinen. "I'm thinking there would be an opening there for old Mea Culpa when this job finishes. It would be right into his barra."

"Cripes!" said Ginger. "Could you see the Mea Culpa catching a randy tom, and thumping his chest as he ran. He couldn't even pull him away from his milk, never mind pull him up the sleeve of a jacket."

After a while somebody remarked, "By the way it must be near opening time."

Opening time was pub opening time, where everybody adjourned to, on a wet day. By right they should stay on site until midday, to qualify for the guaranteed wet time, but nobody bothered, especially when there were no prospects of getting anything done.

"Half an hour yet," I said, checking my watch.

"Look out Pat," warned Tinen, looking over my shoulder. "Somebody is coming to see you."

I looked round, to observe Long Mulholland coming down between the tables towards us. We knew him of old, as we had worked together on various contracts in the past. He was one of the long-distance kids, and had just started that morning. As I was the charge hand timber man, he would have been told to report to me. He was a tall man, over six foot, and a character as well. He was a fine-looking young fellow when I first met him, over twenty-five years before. He would have been about twenty-six then. He was born on Tyneside, of Irish parents, but his long pilgrimages to the old country in his youth left him without any accent. It would go hard on the stranger to pin down where he came from.

"Ha, ha," said he, as he nudged Tinen along the stool. "Move up there Tinen, one would think you were putting on weight, the room you take up. How do timber man? You couldn't cut a stick out off a hedge." And with a big grin he gives Tom a slap on the back.

"Fluke off," protested Tom, haunching his shoulders.

"How are you Pat?" he asked me, as he glanced over his shoulder. "Them bloody card players would drive you up the wall. So they would, with their arguing, and grumbling over a few pennies. Japers! You would think they were playing for pounds. That bloody steam man Docherty has just buggered up ganger Murphy's hand, him with the fingers and all. Good job Docherty is on the other side o' the fence, or he would be down the road on the first chance. By the way Pat, do you remember Holy Dai the Welsh gangerman, up in Warrington long ago? For Wimpey was it not? Well I just heard that the poor fellow is dead."

"I remember him well, and sure who wouldn't. What happened him, as he was not an old man?"

"Oh he is dead over a month now, the big 'C' I think, when that gets a grip on you it's the office for your lying time to be sure, for that cancer is a bugger.

"By japers boys, but he was some Bible thumper, was Dai. A real holy joe if ever there was one, whatever mob he belonged to. Everyone was addressed as 'thee' and 'thou' by him. That is, until one day a bloke by the name of Lyons got him by the throat, and shook him like a rat, shouting, 'Don't you de-dow me you bloody bastard, I'll pulverise you, you antichristic twat. I'll send you to meet your maker before you have time to bless yourself, and it won't be to bloody Wales either.' I think he jacked after that."

"Oh yes," I agreed. "He was a queer one sure enough, and it's a pity he is gone. One of the old characters. As long as you listened to his spouting you didn't have to do anything. Sure the boys in his gang played hell on him, pretending to be all ears, and asking him stupid questions. You would think they were all a bunch of heathens before he came along as a kind of second Messiah. Every bloody one of them standing around with their mouths open, and their shovels going rusty. When he sacked the Spider for calling him a c——t, he told him, 'Get ye out them gates, and dont thee dare look back, for I'll turn thee into a pillar of cement.' The Yank Brown, who was working there at the time remarked, 'Gee whiss! I sure heard of a pillar o' salt, but I aint heard of a pillar o' cement.' I think he would have a hard job turning the Spider into anything other than a pub."

Now as Mulholland rose to go for a slash, it dawned on me, that no doubt he was broke. He knew well we were all carrying, as we had been on site awhile, so he was OK for the sub. Quite a common practice among our kind.

"What are we doing here Pat?" he asked me as he resumed his seat.

"It's going to be a sorting office for the post office when they get round to it. Of course we will be long gone by then, as we are only concerned with the foundation, which you seen as you came in, it goes down quite a bit. Sixty feet to be exact. We are also raking the perimeter piles, and underpinning the north wall to a depth of thirty feet. Deep for underpinning, Mull!"

"By crikey you can say that again, but what is the segment shaft, over in the corner, for?"

"Oh! That was Mowlem's, the company that worked there before we came in," answered Tinen. "They went down to the post office's own little tube line that distribute mail around the sorting offices, and widened the running tunnel to take a platform. We are now going down on it in a square formation to form a lift shaft. More than likely Pat will have you on that tomorrow, if it's dry."

"That will be your station sure enough." I smiled. "It will keep you below ground level, out of sight, for you stand out like Nelson's Pillar on top. One wouldn't mind if you were a bit mobile."

"Piss off! I'm as mobile as this git Tinen anyday. However, that should be a doddle, as we have the segment shaft to strut off, as we sink."

"Where did you hail from now, Mull?" asked Tinen.

"I just pulled out of Southampton. We were sinking a cofferdam there for the cementation. A dirty-old job too. The Long Paton was there, he was last Wednesday anyway. He is some crack the Paton. When you or I place a frame of timber down in a hole, we generally plumb from the frame above. Not so the Paton. Every frame has to be plumbed from the top one. It's like asking a bricklayer to plumb every line of bricks from the foundation. Silly really. Nevertheless he is one of best timber men around.

"I'll tell you about the time he started as a charge hand on this job in Wales. They were sinking a shaft, and well down when he came along. First thing he did was to squint down the hole, with one eye shut. Checking for plumb he was, and whatever he saw didn't please him, for he went rooting in his donkey coat pockets for a plumb bob. All he could find was a head of cabbage, two potatoes, an onion, and a length of string. Cool as you like, he just tied the string to the onion, and lowered it down the hole. After the plumb settled, he shouted down, 'Half a thumb here.' Back came the reply: 'Half a thumb here too.' 'OK,' said Paton, as he began to wind in the string. Now one of the lads below had noticed the onion, and for pure devilment took a bloody big bite out of it. When Paton pulled it up, he just stared at it. 'It's coming to something now,' said he, 'when they're eating into a man's tools.'"

"I once worked with him on a job outside Manchester," said Jim Carney. "He jacked in when they decided to use steel whalings instead of timber. You see they could weld the steel to the piles, so there were no need for puncheons or rakers. Anyway Paton packed in, saying that he was no bloody steel erector."

"I don't know about steel frames being better than timber," said Mull. "Maybe more convenient from the contractor's point of view, less cluttering up, and a clearer field of work, but remember one thing, steel gives no warning of impending doom. Timber will. Many a man's life was saved by creaking timbers. Ask any coal miner. Timber gives you time to get the hell out of it, or strengthen it with extra shores. Steel will not. As for the contractors, all shoring is a nuisance to them, a necessary evil. If they thought for a minute they could get away without it, they would try, as we have witnessed often before. Give me timber every time I say."

We all agreed with him there, as no timber man likes steel shoring.

"There was another man on that job," said Carney. "A man called the Lighthouse Kelly. Did any of you know him?"

"I knew him well," said Mull and I simultaneously.

Mull continued. "He came from one of the islands off the west coast I believe. His father being the lighthouse keeper there, hence the nickname."

"I worked with him after Manchester," continued Carney. "On a dam at Pitlochry, in Scotland. A Wimpey contract. We were timbering a deep trench in shaley rock. Dangerous stuff, as we were going down about a hundred foot. However as Pitlochry was a pretty backwoods kind of a place to accommodate over two thousand men, they ran buses to Perth. Dundee and Glasgow at weekends.

"This Sunday night when the bus crowd arrived back in camp, the Lighthouse was among them, having been to Dundee. He had been seen there by some of the lads, and so the crack started. Now to put you in the picture, there happened to be an old whore knocking about there, by the name of Legless Meg. She was well known to all, including the police. Apparently the poor old thing got herself caught up in the bombing of Clydebank, by the Germans, during the war, and she got blown up. Resulting in the loss of both her legs. Some wag said at the time, that it was not to be wondered at, as no doubt she had her skirt over her head at the time, so the Germans couldn't miss.

"However she was fitted with a new pair, made of tin, which didn't stop her from plying her trade around Dundee afterwards. Glasgow becoming too hot for her. Anyway she came from around Dundee.

"Now it so happened that some of the boys had seen the Lighthouse in her company, in some pub on the Saturday night, and told the rest about it, hence the ribbing: 'Did she unscrew the legs?' … 'Did she leave them standing in a corner or shove them under the bed?' … 'Was she just a low-down bum?' and so on.

"The Gambler McGowen, who never left the camp as he was forever gambling, was in the next bed to the Lighthouse. So he decided to put his spoke in too. 'I suppose Lighthouse you lit her up.' He chuckled, as he turned on his side, to face him. 'Ach hell!' said the Lighthouse. 'You bloody lot wouldn't know a good thing when you saw it. Safest place I ever was. Timbered right up to the arse.' When you knew the Lighthouse, you had to laugh at that."

"They say he was a good dancer in his time," said Mull.

"No, no," I said. "You are mixing him up with the Dancer Kelly, a different man altogether. He was the dancer, and by crikey he could dance. We were once rained off in Bolton, and in the Hen and Chicken. The landlady there had been on the stage one time as a tap dancer. Kelly asked her about it. She told him she gave it up as she was getting too old for it. 'What do you mean too old!' asked Kelly. 'You are not forty yet, look at me, over sixty.' With that he jumped onto the middle of the floor, and started to dance. By japers he showed her some fancy steps. With a stick he burrowed from an old fellow, to use as a cane, he was like that Fred Astaires you hear about. The landlady was so amazed at seeing a scabbyarse navvy in hobnail boots knocking sparks out of her concrete floor, that she stood a round for all of us."

"Ach! He was nothing but a blanket tramper," growled Jim Carney, who once fell out with him.

There was another uproar away behind us at the twenty-five school.

"What's up Dick," asked Ginger of an onlooker, who seemed to be in stitches laughing.

"Ach! It's the steam man again," came the answer. "He has just hammered Murphy's jack o' trumps with the five. Murf is going mad, swearing he is going to have a word with the steam boss about him. Reckoning he should be at work—the rain don't get into the cab of a machine—instead of sitting here, leaving greasy fingermarks all over the cards. Seeing as he never washes his hands, he reckons there is no doubt but his backside must be smuthered in blackjack."

"I think it is opening time. Who is coming for a pint?" I asked.

"We will all go," somebody answered. "The rain is on for the day anyway."

"We will go to the Hog for a bit of peace," said Tinen. "It's a bit further away but them cardsharps won't bother us, as they go to the Crown. More room there and the landlord don't mind the gambling as long as it is kept within limits."

We all agreed. So away we went at a jogtrot against the storm. All except Mulholland, who just moseyed along at his usual steady gait. Rain, hail, or snow, it was all the same to him, as he often said: "Take plenty no notice. I'm in no hurry to go nowhere."

The Hog was not a large house, but the landlord was, and like any man with an eye to business he had an eye to the weather too, so we found him all smiles today. It is not every day a publican finds a large contract on his doorstep. Many a man made his fortune from contracts of a few years' duration. I knew such a man in a small Scottish town who became a millionaire over a six-year contract period. He had the grace to accept the navvy when other publicans there didn't, and God graced him by plonking nearly two thousand of them on his doorstep. Those were the days when no man drank beer on its own.

We ordered our drinks, and retired to a table in a quiet corner, digesting the hypocritical tut-tuts of the landlord regarding the weather.

"Tis an ill wind that don't blow good for somebody," muttered Mull, as he took a swallow from his pint.

More men were now drifting in from our site, and some from another little site round the corner. Soon the place would be crowded, that's why we opted for the corner.

There were six of us at the table. Mull, Ginger, Carney, Tinen, and myself. Also another old-timer by the name of Malone who was already on the perch before we came. He was seated tight up in the corner, making room for as many as possible round the table. More pints for him as everyone knew he was off hire, and dossing down somewhere locally. Of course seeing the weather, and knowing the score, he knew where to find us.

Young Bob now joined us, having refused to participate in a game of darts, preferring our crack.

"Strange the attraction a pub has for the working man," said Mull. "I suppose the toffs use their clubs as their employment exchange, and information centre. Just as we use the pub. A man would be going about scratching his arse if it weren't for them." He forgot to mention that the pub was also a place where one could raise a stake, providing he managed the latchlifter first.

"It's the blooming ruination of us all, so it is," said Ginger. "You have to have money to enter one, to get work, to make money to spend in one, it's like the dog chasing his tail."

"Oh, the pub is all right," I said, "providing you stay clear of the top shelf, the gantry as you might say. A pint of beer never done the working man any harm."

"Neither does the top shelf if taken in moderation," said Malone. Moderation to the same man would be in the region of a bottle o' Scotch. That is, if he could lay his hands on it.

"When on the road, and hitting a town, the ale house is the only place where you get to know what's going on about, and find a place for the liedown," said Mull.

"Oh, true enough Mull," said Malone. "Being on the road has its hazards. Do you remember the Pee Gallagher?"

"Of course, we worked together as often as there is fingers and toes on me."

"What I was going to tell, was about the time he landed in Preston on tramp, with a galoot of a young fellow in tow. They were after jacking on some job up in Shap. So the Pee hit the road. By dad didn't the young rip decide to tag along too. Pee didn't want him atall, as we all know that a man can get along better on his own than with company, and Pee knew his way around. This did not escape the young fellow, so he stuck to him like glue.

"After a few days or so we find them seated in the Coach and Horses, in Preston, with only the price of a few pints between them. Things were looking very grim, and the Pee was deep in thoughts, when the young buck returned from the toilets, looking like a ghost. 'What the hell's wrong with you?' Pee asked him. 'Cripes! there was a bloke in the prowie there, who wanted me to pull him, for ten bob.' 'Did you do it?' 'Not on your bloody life.' 'Damn and fluke you,' said Pee. 'For ten bob I'd pull him from here to Manchester.'"

That brought the laughter. Ginger and Bob nearly had a fit.

"By japers, but ten bob was a fortune in them days," laughed Mulholland, "and the poor old Pee was hungry."

"Serious though," continued Malone, "it's not easy to get rid of a leech once it gets ahold of you. The Dogman o' Dwyre was telling me about what happened to him once when on tramp. A young fellow clamped on to him too. It was at the backend of the year when things are not too lively, and there were little doing anywhere. They were making their way from Nottingham to the Smoke, and it was getting chillier day by day. The Dogman was fed up with the young fellow as he had to do all the begging. Knocking on doors and such. Even when they hit town, it was the Dogman who found any shillings that were going, and that had to do two of them. Let me put it in the Doggy's own words: 'Oy was at the end of my tether about what to do with him, bar shouldering him under a bus, for he was downright useless. One day as we were approaching Biggleswade, and starving with the hunger, with nothing in the kitty, I spied this little farm cottage up a long lane and well off the beaten track. So I thinks to myself, she won't get many beggars up there, I'll give her a try. "I'll wait for you," said my brave buckoo, plonking himself down on the edge of a dry drain, chewing a blade of grass. I went to the back door, and tapped on it nice and gentle like. Moy Jases! It was opened by the ugliest thing I've ever clapped eyes on. She had a face that would curdle honey, with an eye in her head that was neither looking at you or on you, but over your shoulder. "What do you want," she barked at me. I was watching the old spotted hanky she had wrapped round her head, for I didn't know what else to look at. "Well Mam I haven't eaten for two days. I wonder if you could spare me a morsel of something," I said. She screeched at me. I thought for a minute she was going to belabour me with the brush she held in her hands. "Get to hell out of here or I'll call the police, you hairy-faced vagabond." And with that she slammed the door in my face. Japers man, what a name to call a person, and I with only one day's growth on my face. I could see she was connected to the phone as there were two wires tied to the chimney. So I went my way. Damn it now, as I was passing a little extension built to the back of the house, which must have been the kitchen, for on the windowsill rested this huge sweet pie in a tin dish. It was there to cool for the hubby's dinner no doubt. Now with the mighty hunger that was upon me, and smarting from the name she called me, I got to thinking. The man that would marry a treeroot like that deserved neither sympathy nor dinner. So I grabbed the pie, shoved it under my donkey coat, and made off down the lane as fast as my weak legs would carry me. The young rip was still in the drain when I got there, and you should have seen the two eyes of him when he saw the pie. They nearly jumped out of his big red head. By heavens that pie was good. I never tasted anything better. Regardless of her looks she could bake, which showed she was good for something. "Cripes! That was a good poy," said the galoot, as he rubbed his belly, and wiped his mouth with the back of his freckled paw. "Was she not the decent woman for giving it to us." At that I got to thinking perhaps something as good as the pie could come out of this crack. "Oh, she was a grand woman sure enough," I said casual like, as I began filling my pipe. "So seeing as I did the asking the least you can do is to take the tin back, and thank her." "By japers so I will," said he as he jumped to his feet, grabbed the tin, and made for the house. No doubt he was thinking she might give him something else to eat. Once out of sight I made off across the fields, so he couldn't catch me staying on the road. I never seen neither sight nor hair of him since. Though coming to think of it, as I neared the road again in the suburbs of Biggleswade, a police van went belting out the road in yon direction, with its bell clanging. I don't think that playboy will ever again latch on to an old-timer for a meal ticket,' said Pee. Now was that not a terrible trick to play on anybody."

"I think it will be a long time before that lad will eat a sweet pie again," said Young Bob.

There was a bit of a commotion at the bar. Somebody had thrown a punch at somebody else, and that somebody along with the puncher were being railroaded towards the door.

"It's them scaffolders," said Carney. "They have been arguing all week about some bonus they were due. It's that Dublin bloke who hit the deck. I wonder who flattened him."

"Big Jock I think," said Bob.

"Makes no odds now they are both barred," said Ginger. "Sure it's the site agent they should be hitting, and not each other, if it's bonus they are on about."

"True enough," I said. "I remember being in Jersey, one of the Channel Islands, a long time ago. We were doing a tunnel for Kinear Moodie. It was to be a big job, six faces going at the same time. This was at the very beginning of it. However after breakfast one Monday morning—it would be a Monday—we decided to ask the agent for a bigger price per ring. He turned us down flat. So we adjourned to the local, to talk about it! The pub is a great place for discussions.

"After a few hours of debate we decided to have a more diplomatic go at it. So we assembled outside the gate to decide who we would elect to negotiate on our behalf. Eventually we decided that Big Cadwillis would be the best man for it. Cad was a Liverpudlian and an ex-wartime commando. He was one hell of a great bloke in every way. He did not want to do it, but after a bit of persuasion he agreed. So we all stood about awaiting the outcome. We didn't have long to wait, I can assure you, for suddenly from the direction of the office there came a rumble like far-off thunder, to be followed by one almighty blast of splintering wood and glass. Out from where the office window used to be, came a cloud of dust, broken glass, and floating papers. With the site agent flying spread-eagle in the centre of it all.

"We stood there dumbfounded.

"When the dust settled the agent was to be seen sitting on his backside among the rubble, holding his head. He looked stunned. Then slowly from the ragged hole in the wall a big boot appeared, followed by a long leg. The poor agent didn't wait to see any more, he made off like the hammers of hell. For a man that seemed stunned a few seconds earlier he showed a mighty power of recovery, for he passed us doing about fifty. Somebody remarked, 'Maybe Cad wanted to talk outside.' Needless to say we were on the boat back home that night, and everybody as drunk as a puggy."

"I must say," said Mulholland, "you elected a fine diplomat, picked for his tact, no doubt." He laughed.

"The people that represents union folk and such," said Ginger, "are more often than not as thick as two planks, and that's a fact. They get elected because they can talk. That's why you find so many Dubliners and Glaswegians shop stewards on big sites."

"You remind me of a story once told me by a fellow called Melly," said Malone. "Who was a Donegal man same as yourself Pat. He said he was working on this power station up in Darlington where the steward was a Dublin man. A right one too, he said. There were also on site a pair of clowns who worked for a subbie by the name of Gool, who had a contract for digging a rake of holes all over the place. To save supervision costs, he told them they would have to take the dig on piecework. Telling them he wanted their price, per cubic foot, that evening.

"The pair of playactors were stuck, for before they could make out a price they had to know what a cubic foot was. Eventually they agreed that the man for them was Mr Brains himself. Dub the shop steward.

"It took them all day to find him, as his was a powerful busy man. When they did, they asked him, 'Dub, can you tell us what's a cubic foot?' He stared at them for a while, scratching his head, before answering. A sure sign of a good union man. 'Be dads and oy don't know,' he answered, 'but it sounds like a bloody good compensation claim.' Now what do you make of that."

"A typical Donegalman's yarn," said Mull, looking at me. "Never heard one of them tell the truth yet."

We all laughed. The crack was getting better. Could be the beer.

"I for one don't doubt it atall." said Tinen. "For there are some stupid buggers in our business sure enough, yet you can find the odd intellectual too. You wouldn't believe that I once knew a chap on site who was a doctor, or he was near enough being one. It came to light when he saved a man's life, for the man would have been a goner only for him."

"I think I know who you're talking about Tom," I said. "He was a Scot, came from somewhere in the Highlands, Inverness I think."

"You are quite right, Pat, he was from there. I didn't know him that well, just spoke to him in the wet-canteen now and again, he was a proper gent."

"I was in the camp where he kicked off at our game. What happened was this. He failed his final exam to qualify as a doctor, in Edinburgh University, so he had to do another year. He could have done some hospital work during his summer vacation, but he decided to have a break from it all for a while, just to refresh himself, and also earn enough money to see him through the coming year. His father, an ex–army officer, refused to help him. Assuming I suppose, in his military mind, that it was sheer lack of attention and self-discipline that was the reason for failing. So he came to our hydroelectric scheme, having heard of the good money to be made there.

"Well after he had a crack with the tunnel superintendent, who was so impressed he sent him on our shift as a spannerman. To you who don't know what a spannerman is, he is a driller's mate, but in rock tunnels a driller is called a machineman. So a spannerman is a stepping stone to being a machineman. Now you know! A spannerman's job is a coveted position.

"I can tell you one thing though, that super knew what he was doing when he put him on the face, for he was a great worker. You would think he was cut out for it. A strong buck too. I think he played rugby for his college, for he could drink, swear, and sing a song alongside anyone.

"Eventually the gambling bug grabbed him. We all know camps for what they are. Name the game, and it's there. The crown and anchor being the worst. However to shorten my tale the lad was in a world he never knew existed. More money than he ever saw in his life, or indeed likely to see for a number of years, even after qualifying as a doctor. What he didn't drink he gambled, and what he won on gambling he spent on the weekend jaunts to town. He saved nothing.

"The outcome of all this was his refusal to return to college when the time came to do so. Even our persuasion, and coaxing fell on deaf ears. His mind was made up and that was that. Providence made navvies of us, but he was becoming one by choice. A tragedy.

"When he heard that his parents were coming to see him he jacked, and went to work on a neighbouring contract as a machineman, under a different name. He was well liked and well known. We cover our own.

"So his poor mother had to go home empty-handed you might say. I would say she bore no blame. I would definitely put it all on the father. Those military idiots think their family are military personnel, with no mind of their own, and to be treated accordingly. They are incapable of thinking any other way, bringing the barrack square right into their living room. No doubt it was the mother's persuasion that encouraged him to be a doctor or something like that, against the father's wishes for a military career. Well as we are all aware, time passes, men may come, and men may go. Some fade into the mist of antiquity as others stay in mind, contracts finish, and contracts start. Five years were to pass before I was to see the Doc again. We always called him Doc.

"It was in Killin on another hydro job. I was with a friend in the wet-canteen having a drink, when I spotted among the surrounding faces—most of which I knew—a bearded one, that looked sort of familiar. Then I got it! It was the Doc. By hicky! hadn't he changed, for he looked a real hard nut. His black hair was matted, with a thick black beard to go with it. A small scar over one eye, and a front tooth missing. He wore a faded plaid shirt tucked carelessly into a pair of corduroy trousers, held in the up position by a heavy leather belt, buckled to the side manfashion. I called him. He stared at me for a while, before recognition broke across his broad face in a wide grin. He excused himself, and came towards me behind a large outstretched paw, which I warmly shook. We had a good night of it, talking about Tummel Falls where he started, and the men that made it. We parted at closing time, and I never seen him since.

"Afterwards I found out he had a wild reputation for drinking, and fighting, which I believe he was quite handy at. I often wonder what became of him. Often I thought of him being in some pub, and getting into an argument with one of those town gents. The kind that goes through life without learning anything from it. The sort that find it sufficient to judge everyone by their looks. Using their own occupation, with their own consumption of a few halfs of bitter, as a yardstick. The Doc when I seen him last, had lost all his cultured accent, and you would be hard put to say whether he was Highland or Irish. One can just imagine the tactical backsliding of those characters, their slick change of subject on realising they had grabbed a thorn. This is something I found them experts at. Our way is to take a man as he comes, for none of us is clever enough to know it all."

"By heaven Pat you said a mouthful there," said Mull. "For among our ranks I have known a lawyer, he had been in jail for a spell. A spoiled priest, an ex-monk, and one Jesuit, who was a bad bastard. There is room for all of them among us. Immune from the rest of the world, a refuge for the infected, far from the cares there are, among the damned. This happy breed. When did you hear of a navvy throwing himself under a train or such? In London it's a kind of a failing they got. Two a week jumping under trains. You may find a navvy dead, aye dead drunk no doubt. Nothing that a night in the calaboose won't put right. He walks the road alone, and cherish the right to do so. Sleeps under the stars when compelled to. Drink to the past, but never the future. Sings of what was, never what is. Court a wench when found willing, and damn the world that damns him in turn. He who has given them roads with bridges. Power with dams, and tunnels for their trains, not to mention sewers to piss in. We the untouchables. They would rather shoot their daughters than allow them to marry one of us. Hell! Who could blame them."

"By japers Mull you are on your soapbox today right enough," said Malone. "It's speaker's corner for you next stop."

"Ach! I do get carried away by times when I think about it."

"Never mind," said Ginger. "It's the God's truth, and that's a fact."

He turned to me. "Do you know what I once read, Pat. This doctor was wanted for murder somewhere. I think it was his wife he done in. However, he worked for years among the navvies without being found by the law. Then one day a man was seriously hurt on the job, and so badly injured he would never make hospital without immediate medical attention. The doctor being present obeyed his calling, and seen to him there and then. When they got him to hospital, the doctors there knew immediately that it had to be another doctor who attends him, in spite of assurances that it was the work of a fellow worksman. The outcome was his arrest, and a verdict of guilt returned at his trial, with a strong recommendation for mercy in view of what he had done. He should have been let off, I say. A man like that would kill no one without a damn good reason for doing so, and being a doctor he didn't have to throttle her."

"Doctors are a queer bunch to be sure," said Jim Carney. "Myself, I have seen them on more than one occasion risk life and limb crawling to a trapped and injured man, to give him an injection to ease his pain. Once we had a man trapped under this huge fall, and knew for sure he was as dead as mutton, but we had to stop work to let the doctor crawl in to confirm it. It was touch and go getting himself out alive afterwards."

"When you talk about doctors," said Malone with a twinkle in his old eye. "The Long Dogherty was telling me about a time when he was in digs somewhere in the West Country. It was during the war years when grub was rationed. His old landlady, or so he reckoned, fed him on nothing but rabbits, which were plentiful in that part of the country. Rabbit stew, rabbit pie, rabbit sandwiches, and rabbit soup made from the bones. Eventually he became very ill, and broke out in an almighty rash. The landlady fearing he might have the plague or something, you couldn't tell with navvies, sent for the doctor. The doctor looked at him, and asked the madam what medicine she administered. 'Oil. Castor oil, two big spoonfuls,' answered the besom, with a 'Hum!' Old Dogherty looked up at the doctor, from what he was sure was his death bed. 'Listen Doctor,' he managed to croak. 'It's not a doctor I want atall but a fucking ferret.' He got better."

We were in stitches, especially Young Bob, and he didn't even know the Long Dogherty. If he did, he would have choked.

"That," I managed to splutter, "reminds me of Martin Mees when he was in digs, and his landlady fed him on nothing but fish. Granted the place was Grimsby. Martin got fed up with it, and decided to flit. Mind you everything was in order, digs paid right up. As he was going out the door, she nabbed him, and chastised him for going without telling her. Then asked him where he was going, no doubt hoping she would know the place, and put the sprag in for him. 'I'm going up the river to spawn,' said Martin, and he made off."

Ginger was now getting quite merry as he always did after a few pints. He could sing a good song too, when he was in the mood. He turned to me now smiling. "Pat I'll tell you something," he said. "There was a man working with me up in Grangemouth who lived in Glasgow, like most of the men on site—it being a Lilly's job—he commuted daily, as Lilly ran a bus for them. This man was a fitter by the name of Barney."

"Not interrupting you Ginger," broke in Mull, "but I knew Barney well, and when you're finished I'll tell you something about him. Carry on."

"Well Barney was telling about a character back in Glasgow City who worked for the corporation, on house drains, street repairs, and things like that. His gangerman was one Hughie O'Donnell, a very dour man whose wife kept a lodger for many years, until he went and died on her. Some malicious neighbours said it was the hunger he died with, which was all wrong. After a respectable time had passed, or at least long enough to stop the same neighbours from saying she should have let the bed go cold before flogging it again, she asked the husband if there were anybody on his job needing good digs.

"The long and short of it was that Hughie landed home with this clouster in tow, as a potential lodger. Whether it was his own decision or the ganger's, we will never know. Sufficient to say galoots found work hard to get in them days. Now the digs were good no doubt about it. What the landlord ate you ate, and that can't be bad.

"Every night after they had a wash in the jawbox, they sat down at the table, which was already set for them. Nice and clean like, with a big dish of potatoes in the centre. The governor sat at the top, of course. Thus they waited for what she and the good Lord would provide in the form of meat and veg. It was while waiting so, that our man the clouster noticed the potato dish was loaded against him. Just like a dice. All the big spuds were stacked on the governor's end of the dish while the little ones were crowded at his end. Had they been peeled one wouldn't mind atall, but being in their jacket was a different proposition entirely. By the time you had a skitter of small spuds peeled, your opposite had the best wolfed down at his ease. He thought a lot about this state of affairs, and spent quite some time pondering about a remedy for it. He didn't want to move as that meant job as well, so he took it to bed with him. Then it struck him, a plan that could be implemented right away.

"The following evening while at the table awaiting the nosebag, he remarked quite casual like, 'I was reading in the paper, Hughie'—the ganger was *Hughie* at home—'this astronomer reckons that the world goes round.' 'What do you mean round,' asked Hughie. 'Just like that,' said our man, catching the potato dish, and giving it a quick half turn. The old fellow was watching the dish for a while before asking, 'Are you an astronomer?' 'No. No I'm not.' 'Then leave the frigging world as it is,' said he, as he grabbed the potato dish, and turned it back to its original position. Over and out! The owld fellow wasn't made a ganger for nothing."

We laughed at that.

"No doubt," said Ginger, after gathering his composure. "Hughie made sure that the buck was left with little time for any further scheming, the following day."

"Getting back to Barney," said Mull, "and forgetting that clouster of a lodger. Any man who takes a ganger home with him deserves all he gets. Anyway I always thought they put gangers in the toolbox at the end of the day, along with other implements. After all, Dracula sleeps in a box!

"But talking about Barney, we worked together in Shrewsbury on a tunnel job some years ago. He was a great man for writing songs and verses. I think he had some published. However there was an old girl who used to hang about the site entrance every day. She never spoke, just came and went. She seemed pleased to be allowed to watch what was going on at the pithead. All the lads were naturally very good to her, and were forever giving her empty beer bottles—of which there were always plenty about—pieces of timber for her fire, and money too.

"Somebody christened her 'Diesel Mary', as she used to sit on an empty diesel barrel that lay by the gates. Barney was in such a melancholy mood one Monday morning, after getting the cure, which he needed badly, having been home to Glasgow for the weekend, that he wrote a little poem about her. I'll give it if I can remember it all, for it was a while ago now.

'The first time I saw my Diesel Mary.
I was building a gantry at Longden Green,
Her curls were matted, her face was hairy.
And the neck below it was far from clean.
Charlie Henry was frying bacon.
His brother Domhnal was brewing tay.
As she lingered around the doorway.
Arrah Diesel Mary will you go away.
Like a faithful collie she wouldn't leave us.
But came to see us nine times a day.
We gave pages, and bits of sleepers.
And empty bottles to take away.
We knew she liked us, but gave no token.
If her heart was breaking, she didn't say.
Yarrah Mary darling I would take it easy.
For one fine morning we'll be all away.
The job was done, and the summer over.
The team grew smaller day by day.
One to Bournmouth, and one to Bolton.

And one to labour beyont the Tay.
Where the shaft was yawning, the grass grow over.
Where the gantry hovered small children play.
Little the know of Diesel Mary.
Or the wayward miners who could not stay.'

Everybody was quiet for a while after that. "Now," continued Mull. "What do you think of that?"

"There is a lot of meaning in a simple little verse, even when made in fun," said Malone.

"There's the last bell," said Ginger, as he finished his beer.

"It's up and away as the sailors say," added Carney. "I suppose tomorrow will be wet again, please God."

"Speak for yourself," said Mull. "I need a few shillings."

We all finished our drinks, and with a cheerio here, and there went our ways. Wondering if tomorrow would be wet.

Chapter 2

It was snowing hard and it was lying, which presented a bleak outlook on the first day of December. Rain to the ground worker is just a passing phase, here today and gone tomorrow, but the shroud of white with its brother frost is a different kettle of fish altogether. That we might be rained off for quite a while, so early in the winter, were the thoughts passing through many minds as we watched it pile up on the canteen windowsills.

Strange how falling snow seems to kill all sound, I was thinking. The heaviest footstep on the roughest of gravel is as mute as the cheerful chirp of the songbird.

Conversation was sparse within the canteen. The most noise came from the card players, and that was sober by standards. Nobody cherished the thoughts of being on the slagheap so near to Christmas. Perhaps things would cheer up when the pubs opened.

"I doubt if it will lie," muttered Mulholland as he cleaned a patch of fogged-up window, and peeped out. "There's too much heat still in the ground in spite of that cold rain we been having. Still I've known it to come just as early, and stay for long."

Nobody answered him.

"Do you know," said a man called McDaid, yawning, "they get heavier falls of snow in Yorkshire than they do in the Highlands of Scotland. I've seen a drift of snow a hundred foot deep, at a place called Cunning corner, in Yorkshire. They had to blast it away eventually."

"I've read about that," I said. "They get it heavy, but they don't get it as persistent as they do in the Highlands. Rarely does the snow lie in the Lowlands. Up North they pass very little comment on snow as they know it is inevitable, and are well prepared for it. Every vehicle has a set of chains in its toolbox, and carries a shovel. Even the trains are fitted with snow ploughs when winter approaches. Catch the dour Scot.

"Oh contraptions like that are a help," said Mulholland as he pulled on his short pipe, his long legs stretched right across the passageway and his back propped against the wall.

Here we go for a crack to lift the gloom, I thought to myself.

"I was once working with a small contractor in Perthshire when the white stuff came," he continued, "being just a small firm they could not afford wet-time over a long period, so we would eventually be paid off. That is, until the thaw came.

"On the morning it started, we were moved from the site to their nearby yard, thus enabling us to get our day in. We would be stood down that evening—should the snow persist—and be fully paid up. Those little firms were quite good.

"Anyway as we messed about having the crack, we were quite happy as there were only six of us, and being inside a big shed out of the blizzard with a blazing brazier of coke beside us, we hadn't a care in the world. We also knew there would be plenty casual work with the council over the next few days, shovelling snow. More about that later.

"This little firm had but one lorry on the road, an old square-nosed Bedford which was driven by an old blockhead of an ex-ploughman called MacCutchen, who was now messing about with the engine. At least he had the bonnet up, perhaps hiding behind it to avoid being sent along with us cleaning and greasing tools.

"To put you in the picture regarding this firm, it appeared the founder had snuffed it a week or two back, and left it all to his son and daughter, though MacCutchen maintained he didn't leave it, but was taken away from it. The family had been running it for years anyway, the son on the outside, and her in the office. They were no youngsters as they were both in their forties. People said that she was the boss, and the dead spit of the old bastard, and by local gossip he had been all that. Tales were told about him going about wearing a bowler hat, and poking men in the ribs with his umbrella while telling them to get a move on. Had I been there. I know where the umbrella would be poked, and it wouldn't be up his nose. MacCutchen now due for retirement, had been with them for donkey's years, and had detested the old man. I believe the feeling was mutual, and only for the son he would have been fired years ago. Perhaps he was one of those poked.

"However this day, as we got stuck into our little tasks, didn't herself appear in the yard carrying a piece of paper, and hollowing for MacCutchen. He heard her, and went across the yard to meet her, cleaning his hands with a piece of rag as he went. When he came back after a while, his face was grim, and he was cursing. 'Damn yon woman onyway,' she says, 'as ah have nothing te dae, ah can gang te Dundee, and gather the auld coots ashes frae the crematorium. Damn it te hell I'll no make it in yon blizzard. She could have waited fine till the snaw had gang. Christ ashes will no rot.'

"Well we got him away eventually after helping with the wheel chains, and we wished him well.

"At about three o'clock we saw the lorry coming back into the yard smothered in snow. The only clear patch was a quadrant of windscreen by the wiper. Mac dismounted carrying a brown vase, and went straight into the office. For a while things were quiet, nobody paying any attention to the rising voices therein, until there came an almighty screech from that direction, and MacCutchen came tearing out, followed by a flying vase, which caught up with him and bouncing off his head. The clonk of it hitting the skull could be heard a mile away. Such a wallop would have stretched any normal man, but MacCutchen's head was all bone. He just stood there rubbing it with his hand, as he looked around for the vase, which he found in the snow at his feet. He just picked it up and placed it on the doorstep, I thought for a minute he was going to make a rugby ball of it, and give it a garryowen, before he came across to us. Now all this hullabaloo required some explanation, so he was asked to. 'Weel,' he said, rubbing the pow as he glanced over his shoulder towards the office, 'she's no very pleased ye ken, though ah did ma best. Ye a ken the road te Dundee. No! Not the sang man'—some wag had started humming the tune—'but the wey. Ah got there reit enough, and gathered the ashes, it's on the wey back ah got inta trouble. Ye ken yon sharp brae at Kinfauns, it's a fair steep yin, and an awfy drop doon tae the river beneath, with nay railings. Weel ah started skidding halfwey up, and ah was feart ah would gang in the river, so ah used ma loaf. Ah grabbit yon vase that was in the cab, got the top of in a hurry, and slung them ashes under the back wheels. It worked a treat mon, for she grippit right away, and that's how ah got here. Yet yon lassie took a tantrum when she sees the empty vase. Some folk hae nae understanding atall.'

"MacCutchen looked round at his audience, who were now standing there dumbstruck. Then he just threw his head back, and burst into a gale of laughter that infected all of us. We were in stitches. At last he managed to wipe his eyes. 'Fuck him onyway,' he stuttered, 'that's yin day he didna get paid for, the old bastard.' Now what do you think of that for a crack. A nice end to an old man, and a burned one too."

"If the bugger was as coarse in life as the neighbours said, I have no doubt but his ashes were as coarse, and just the job," laughed Tom Tinen.

"Talking about cremations," I said, "there used to be a character about Glasgow named Charlie Freel, who came from my part of the world. He lost a leg under some machine on site, which wondered nobody for he was an awkward clouster at the best o' times. However he got a fair lump of compensation out of it, and decided to go to America as he had some friends there, but then who hasn't. Funny enough most people go there to make money not with money, but then didn't I say he was awkward. What he did there over the years I don't know but he died there, and believe it or not requested to be cremated and his ashes taken back home to be scattered along a local byroad. The bleakest bloody road in the County. It was well named when it was called 'The Moorhen Road'. Why he requested this remains a mystery. Maybe one local was near the truth when he remarked, 'Twas on the making of that road he earned enough to get him out of here, and he never forgot it.' Perhaps so. However when the vase arrived it was met by the two characters that still occupied the old homestead, his kin, Johnny and Nelly. Indeed you wouldn't call either of them wise for they waked the casket for three days and nights, with the odd neighbour calling to pay their respects. If you ask me it was sheer curiosity that brought them, for nobody there had ever seen a cremation urn before. One man called it 'a glorified ash bucket'. Perhaps he was right.

"On the third day the pair got dressed up, took the urn, and solemnly headed for the chosen spot. It was a wild windy day. There, Johnny with more curses than prayers wrestled with the urn's lid, as it was sealed. Eventually he got it opened after giving it a belt or two with a big stone, and started to scatter the ashes. Just as if he was sowing corn. Damn it sure every handful was caught by the wind, and carried away over the moors. A known character living about six miles down wind of them, on hearing about it, blamed it immediately for a stye he got on his eye that same day. The best crack was Nelly's as she turned to a passing cyclist—who had stopped to watch the crack—and remarked, 'God almighty, poor Charlie will be blown to hell,' which he was, literally speaking. But do you know that none of the locals would use that road after dark."

"I suppose being a Yank," said Mull, "he was too miserable to pay for a proper burial at home, probably got a discount from the charcoal burners because of the missing leg. Less to burn do you see."

"I don't blame people for not using that road at night," said Young Bob. I believe in ghosts."

"The only fluking ghost you are ever likely to see young man, is Ryan there," said Mull.

"If I'm a ghost then I don't have to buy a round when we get to the pub at opening time. Japers it's that time already! Come on, whoever is going."

There were a few people in the pub when we entered, the felt-covered floor was already wet, with melting snow. We ordered our drinks, and made for a corner table. There were six us in the company, no doubt a few more would join later.

"The snow will make the governor happy," said Ryan, as he took a good swig from his pint. "Still he will lose in the long run, as we won't be around until it thaws."

"Don't shed any tears for a publican," said Mull, "they are a surviving breed, and seldom go to the wall. They can be caught out of course but damn rarely. I only heard of one that did. He was in Camden Town, and was plagued with flies during a hot summer. I would say that having a pub in Camden Town was a big enough plague in itself. However he offered ten pounds, and a load of drink to anybody who could get rid of them. There were a few attempts at it but none succeeded. Then one day this Herbert landed, and swore that he could do it. The landlord believed him, and gave him a large whiskey. After another two which he explained was for courage, he was ordered to start performing. 'Right landlord,' said he, as he went outside, and tossed off his jacket, then rolling up his shirt sleeves, he struck up a fighting pose. 'Ready sir when you are, just send them out now one at a time, and I'll soon fluken shift them.'

"Needless to say he had to shift pretty fast himself, for the same landlord, though slow in the mind was pretty fast on the feet."

"Ah. Bunkum!" said Ryan. "I've met some clousters in my time but none that daft. I suppose that's one of your own clever ideas."

"Right enough you seldom hear of a landlord going bust," said Tinen. "Any trouble they have always seem to be women trouble. I suppose a man and woman being under each other's feet morning noon and night time, gets on each other's nerves, also the strain of having to be polite to some bastard you could quite easy shoot, were you allowed to."

"I think the North Country publicans are the funniest lot," I said. "I was just thinking there of something that happened long ago. You see I was working in a place called Goostrey in Cheshire, and frequented a little pub on the outskirts of town. It was in the town, and yet not in the town, that kind of a position. A grand wee house. Now it so happened the landlord died, after serving his customers faithfully for a quarter of a century. So his daughter took control. Not a bad lassie, but not a patch on the old fellow.

"The village bobby was an old boy too, who had been there for years, and known to all. So one afternoon when off duty, soon after the old boy died, didn't he call into the bar for a pint, one of his very rare visits. Naturally he got chatting to the girl. 'I fairly miss old Bob,' 'So do I, he was a grand man, one of the best,' went the patter. 'I doubt if we will ever see his like again. Do you know lass, for the last twenty years he always left a pint for me on yon back window's sill, knowing I would be along, doing my nightly rounds. Aye he was a grand man.' 'Was that pint for you!' she exclaimed. 'My oh my! And he always told me last thing at night, to fill a pint out of the slops bucket, and leave it out there for the birds.' That was the end of that crack."

The bar was now full of men, and the ale flowing, as you could tell by the rising tone of conversations. There were no card playing today. I noticed Big Rab MacGillian among them, and taking up the space of three men. The huge donkey coat he wore, made him look like a bear. Ginger reckoned that his wife was just as big, and the donkey coat was originally bought for her, to stop her pestering him for a coat. The fur variety she had in mind. She should have taken it for it would be the nearest thing to a fur coat she was ever likely to get. He had the reputation of being the fastest pint drinker in the country. Twas true that he had no swallow. A story went about that he was in the cab of a wagon passing through Melton Mowbray once, when they were held up at the traffic lights. There was a pub at the corner with the doors wide open. Rab jumped out and nipped in, ordered and paid for a pint, drank it, and was back in the cab before the lights changed. He appeared to be with a bloke called "Sweedie the Chippie" today. A wee runt of a man with quarter-to-three feet, and a compulsive yapper. How Rab got mixed up in his company, I'll never know.

"Do you remember back in the canteen when I was telling you about Perth, and the snow," said Mull, nodding in Bob's direction. "I said there would be more to say about it later. Well seeing Big Rab there reminded me, as he was with me at the time.

"That winter turned out a bad one for we were laid off for over a month, and had to go on the snow clearing, while it lasted. That was a big operation in Perth in those days, and they went about it in style. Over two hundred men employed as casual labour to keep the streets clear. The ploughs pushed it into the kerb so they could load it on wagons, to be dumped in the River Tay. You started at the council yard in the morning by signing on the dotted line, with no questions asked as you were dished out a shovel. Now that was no ordinary shovel, it was your identity card, your pay chit, and your bread and butter all in one. For you see, without the shovel you did not get paid. Only when you handed it over at the end of the shift did they pay you. Wherever you went or whatever you did all day, the shovel went too. Without it even the ganger you worked with couldn't help you. So you can just imagine how well the shovel was guarded. Cripes man you dare not let it out of your hands for a minute. You took it to the bog, to the cafe, and any other place you went. In the evening when the lights were low, and dark shadows creeping, the place was alive with creepy-crawly things lurking in dark doorways and sombre closes. Shovel rustlers, waiting like vultures to pounce on a careless victim.

"The council men were in high heaven during this operation, as they were all made acting gangers for the duration. Some went beyond the call of duty, and gave a demonstration of the kind of ganger they would never make, by telling you to get lost, and come back in the evening, hoping you might take them to the pub. There were others who became little Hitlers, hoping to catch the eye of a supervisor, and earn a recommendation for promotion.

"Rab and I were sent with a real bugger of a man, who was normally employed as a scaffy* who was out for all he could get. His area was the Glasgow Road, which was a fairly posh road, and a very busy road, with extra-wide pavements. We were on the pavements, as the traffic kept the road clear. This character had half of us clearing private drives, with himself away ahead of us doing the canvassing, and the collecting. He also had a man posted farther down the road on the lookout for passing supervisor vans. We were doing well, and he was doing well, but we could have done better still, had he not gone and pick the biggest clouster in Perth as a lookout. That bastard jumped at the first offer of a cup of tay, and was sitting smug in somebody's kitchen when the supervisor caught us. We got a bollocking, and a free transfer to another team. The ganger was demoted and sentenced to a place where he could be watched.

"The next ganger we got was an old boy on the verge of retiring, and didn't give two hoots. His task was to clear the back streets. He broke us up into pairs, allotting each pair a certain street, and told us to get on with it. I think he only wanted peace o' mind and to get away to his local.

"Rab and I were allocated a little street called Canal Street, where the footpaths were very narrow, just about two foot. So it didn't take us long to clear a stretch of it. Eventually we decided to leave some for the following day, and go for a few pints, where we stayed till closing time, which was half past two.

"When we came out the streets were deserted, and we had two hours on our hands before shoveling time. It was fierce cold, as we contemplated on how to kill the time. At the end of the street there stood a little cinema called the BB's, which had a threepenny matinee every afternoon, mainly for kids and old-age pensioners, plus the odd dosser. We decided to try to get in. Damn me but we did , and it was cosy and warm.

"You can just imagine the setup. A pair of scruffy navvies in among the truanters, pensioners, and layabouts, with two bloody-big shovels between their knees, watching Donald Duck. I looked at Rab sitting beside

---

* a dustman in Scotland

43

me, his stubbled chin resting on the shovel handle, and him nodding off to sleep. I was in half a mind to creep out later, and leave him there, just to see what would happen when he turned up at the council office with a shovel, near midnight. Christ! he would break the place, and me with it. Well now, as I thought about it, I let out such a roar of laughter, it nearly brought the house down. It was the wrong time to do so, for at that moment they were playing soft music as a lament for a cringing lassie that was about to be made a meal of, by some mangy-looking cur wearing a bloody bonnet, and my outburst fluked it all up. I may not have brought the roof down, but it certainly brought the usher down the aisle, accompanied by some kind of gangerman. First of all they blinded us with a bright flashlamp before ordering us to hell out. I think myself, it was the shovels that were the deciding factor. He told us in no mean terms, that we shouldn't have been let in atall, and that we would not get in again. You would think he was talking about the Ritz. He cooled down a bit when threatened with a shovel decapitation on the spot.

"We spent nearly two weeks on the snow clearing that winter, which was a great help, as we were staying in a local kip, costing sixpence a night. Aye, you may look surprised Young Bob, but that was the charge. Mind you it was not what you would call a five-star hotel, but it did. Now there was a better one in town, but it was full up because of the weather, so with the few bob we got from the snow we were better off than some of the others. I was never back in Perth since, so I suppose that cinema is long gone now, like everything else. It was a nice city—very clean—but if you noticed, most Scottish cities and towns are. Maybe it's the scourge of wind that's constantly passing through. Their cinemas are not much cop though."

"The doorman shouldn't have let you in atall," said Ryan. "If it was me, I'd have sent for the polis, and have you charged. One, having an offensive weapon. Two, defrauding the council of snow money. Three, misuse of public property. It would sound nice in the courthouse: 'The aforesaid culprits, found in possession of council property. To wit, two shovels, issued for the purpose of clearing snow, being used as chin rests while unofficially in a local cinema watching Donald Duck.' Not to mention the ex-colonel-of a-sheriff's remarks about Mull's eyes being too close together for comfort. Three months' hard labour would be about right."

"Did I hear my name being taken in vain," said Big Rab, as he loomed over us. "No doubt Mulholland is at it again."

"Come and join good company," said Mull, as he kicked a chair in his direction. Sweedie was at present annoying somebody else. "Better than the company you were with anyway. That Sweedie would bore you to tears. Where are you working? You have not been around."

"Oh, I'm on that job up the street. The new bank building in Lemore Close. Sweedie is also there. He has a bit of a shout, as good chippies are hard to find nowadays."

"Say, what you like about the Sweed, but he is a good carpenter, and a quick one too," I said. "Mick Conway the subbie was talking about him as he worked for him, and Conway don't employ duds. We all know how contrary he is on occasions, so it won't surprise you when you hear what Conway told me. Apparently next door to Mick lived a bitch of a neighbour, with a dog and cat. All proper pests. She asked Mick once if he could send one of his joiners round to do a little job for her. So to keep the peace Mick agreed, and sent Sweedie along. Damn me, but she had him for three days messing about the house, and he could not get away from her. If it wasn't one thing, it was another. However at long last he managed to finish, or so he thought, and was about to pack away his tools when she corners him again. 'There is one little thing you might do for me before you go, if you wouldn't mind,' she asked. 'You see puss spends an awful lot of his time in the garden, poor pet, and I don't always hear him when he wants to come in. Could you cut a little square out of the back door panel, and hinge it? A cat flap I think they call it. Pussy is very clever and will soon learn to use it.'

"Sweedie dropped his tools on the floor with a clatter. 'If he's that fucking clever,' he growled, 'why don't you get a key cut for him instead.' She wanted no more to do with him, so he left."

"Sweedie had his answers, and no doubt about it," said Ryan. "I heard of him being missing from the job once, when the foreman who was looking for him spotted him coming in the gate. 'Hoy!' he shouted. 'Where the fuck have you been? I've been looking all over the place for you.' 'I've been for a haircut,' answered the Sweed. 'Haircut! All your hair didn't grow on the firm's time.' 'No,' replied Sweedie, 'and I didn't get it all cut.'"

"You could enjoy his company if he could stop talking for a while," said Rab. "Cripes he never ceases, though he comes out with some good yarns now and again. He was telling me about some job he was on, and the charge hand chippy was an old Scotsman. A nice old man, he said, but very excitable. They were shuttering this section of a dam, and had two lads drilling holes in the surrounding concrete, for anchors. Old Jock was trying to explain some detail to the chippies, but could not make himself heard above the din. Eventually it got the better of him, and he went haywire altogether, swinging his rule about, and dog dancing around, roaring for quiet. He hit the drillers on the shoulder, and stopped them on the spot. Now, there were a pair of chippies there, who were dummies, and they were chatting away with their fingers. In his excitement Jock also lashed out at their fingers, shouting, 'That goes for you fuckers too.' The poor fellows were confounded, until they saw the funny side of it, then they joined in the laughter, to Jock's embarrassment."

"By japers," said Mull. "He may have silenced the dummies, but I'm bloody sure he didn't silence the Sweedie. I keep well away from him when I see him coming, with that two feet of his. Like a cow shitting. Forgetting Sweedie though. Is there anything new around Rab?"

"Oh, damn the hate. I don't leave the Smoke much nowadays, not since the squaw got hold of me. Cripes, there is a lot to be said for the tinker and his ashplant. He knows how to keep them in order. If a tinker's wife didn't get a belt of it on a fair day, she would make out there was somebody else, and create such a row that nothing would quieten her but a wallop of it. With a fair chance of a boot up the arse as well. Sound people."

"Aye, they are strange, sure enough," I agreed. "I saw one of them in Aberfeldy once, giving the old hairpin a belt or two with the ashplant, when this young onlooker made for him. He didn't get far, for she ups with a bucket she was carrying, and flattened him with it. I'll bet you he minded his own business after that."

"Aye," said Mull. "They may appear hard on their women, but you tell me if you ever heard of one getting divorced! Never. They are good to them in their own kind of way, and the women don't complain. Another thing, you make a friend of a tinker and you have a friend for life. Many a night I spent among them, and shared a bottle with them, in their roadside shacks. Around that place you mentioned, Aberfeldy, was a great place for them. I believe there are certain pieces of land in Scotland which they used to call 'king's land,' where they can camp for a certain time without being molested. Of course they can be made to moved eventually, under the pretext that they were causing a nuisance, or something like that. Sure the Hen Maughan was a tinker, of the Irish tribe. Quite a few of them gave up the tinkering for our game. Damn it when you look at it there isn't much difference between us."

"How did he get called the Hen?" asked Young Bob. "A very funny name."

"No funnier than the man," laughed Tinen. "He got called the Hen because he was a bit fond of them, and was never satisfied unless there was one in his pot, and don't ask how he could afford it, for he never bought one in his life. He was worse than any fox. Sure if you were on the back of a lorry going to work, or going anywhere for that matter, while you and everybody else were seeing things to talk about, the Hen could see nothing but chicken coops. 'Look at that rake of hen coops,' he would say, licking his chops."

"You never came across a fox like him," added Mull. "He could steal a hen from under the nose of any dog in broad daylight. He explained to me once, how to kill a hen as soon as you catch her. Apparently there's a soft spot in the hen's skull, just under her kurk, so you press your thumb on that, and she's a goner. He also maintained if you put a duck's head under her wing, and rock her twice she falls asleep. Mind you I never tried any of them, but knowing the Hen, I'm sure it's true."

"Did I ever tell you about the time him and I did three months in Perth penny," said Rab.

"Not that I can recall," I said.

"Well we did. As Mull was talking about the snow in Scotland a wee while ago, it so happened that the Hen and I got caught in it one winter, on our way to a place called Crianlarich in West Perthshire. There was a bit o' work going on there at the time, and that's where we were heading when the damn snow caught us going over Glen Ogle, just above Lochearnhead. Strange enough, a deep glen on the top of a mountain and a bare windswept place at that. As it was getting dark when the blizzard hit us, and with a few miles still to go, the Hen suggested we go down into the railway cutting below the road in the bottom of the glen, and there perhaps we might find a railway bothy, to hole up for the night. We got down after one hell of a struggle, and sure enough about fifty yards along the line near the entrance to a tunnel, stood a railwayman's hut. It was a little sleeper house with a table and a few chairs, also a little fireplace. It was quite comfortable after we lit the fire, as there was a stack of coal with some faggots in the corner. Then we lit the paraffin lantern that hung from the rafters, and drummed up. We knew we would not be disturbed as this line closed down on the first hint of snow, so we relaxed, and had a good night's sleep under some sacks we found.

"The following morning there was no letup in the blizzard. It was now about two foot deep on the track, and still blowing down from the surrounding mountains. We weren't afraid of being buried, as there were several shovels in the hut. Our grubstake would last out for a few days, when one of us would have to trudge over the hill to Lochearnhead for some more. Also there was a pack of cards and a draughtboard in the hut.

"Things had gone great guns for a week, the Hen having been for the commodities, but we were running out of coal, and that was our downfall. You see, we were too comfortable, and stayed there too long. Two weeks before a fluking-big steam engine came out of the tunnel, pushing a huge snowplough in front of it, and a gang of railwaymen fussing around it like chicks round a mother hen. Only for that damn tunnel we could have seen them coming, and been off. Not that the railwaymen up in that country would object to anybody taking refuge in one of their huts, but, wait till you hear. The dirty big engine was puffing away fine as she passed by our hut, when suddenly, she gave an almighty lurch, and nose-dived into the snow, to sit there like the Loch Ness Monster, farting and blowing a shower of sparks. As the Hen said later, 'She went down like the Titanic,' and that's the way she went, right off the lines. No wonder, for how do you think we kept our fire going but with the little blocks that keep the rails in their chairs on the sleepers! There weren't one left for a hundred yards on each side of us. All kicked out by the Hen. Needless to say the police were called, and we had no more snow worries for the following nine weeks.

"It was in the courthouse, the Hen compared the sinking of the engine to that of the Titanic. He spoke as if it was some mighty achievement, which the sheriff no doubt took into view."

"You got off lightly with three months," I said. "I suppose having to survive in a blizzard for two weeks was taken into consideration. Survival is the first law of the moors. Methinks that would be the longest stretch the Hen ever did without his fowl. God help the first unfortunate hen that crossed his path on his release, for she would be devoured feathers and all. We were in Doyle's Bar in the Gorbals one day when the Tash Roarty came in, laughing and made the statement, 'I have just seen the Fox Brown coming down the Gallogate with the Hen Maughan in his mouth!' It was hilarious as everybody knew they were mortal enemies."

"There was a tale about him which I heard in Doyle's Bar," said Tinen, "regarding a whore out of that women's Model Lodging House in Carrick Street, and there were some hard cookies staying there. Now you heard of number one Patt Steet, the men's motel that was just round the corner from number 1D. Incidentally a clerk in the wartime Food Office remarked to me once, when applying for a new ration book, that the half of bloody Ireland must be living there. He had a point, for if you only stayed there for one night you could call forever to collect your mail. So it was handy for a fixed abode.

"Anyway, late one night as the Hen was pelting past the end of Carrick Street making for Pit Street, with a loaf of bread under his arm, a whore accosted him to inform him that she had a 'short time' for sale. The Hen said no, as he had no money. I think the standard rate around there at the time was between half a crown and five bob, and dear at that, considering the quality one was getting …"

"You must have been sniffing around there to know the tariff," interrupted Ryan, with a giggle.

"Piss off," retorted Mull. "He wouldn't touch your type of pastime."

Tinen ignored Ryan and continued. "She pointed to the loaf under the Hen's order. 'That will do,' she said. She must have been bloody desperate.

"As the loaf was the Hen's full breakfast, he was loath to part with it, but then again it was tempting. The outcome was the pair of them made for some dark corner known to her, in Carrick Street. Some bombed-out building. It would be worth a fortune if they could have been photographed. The Hen with his cap on the slew as if struck by lightning. The whore, now the owner of the loaf, holding it under her arm. It would have to be pretty stale, if it was to keep any kind of shape or form. However when they were finished, so the story goes, she placed the loaf on the ground, while she tidied herself up. The Hen meantimes had his eye on it, with deep regrets. Breakfast was not that far off, and be dads he was feeling a bit peckish already. Fluke it, he said to himself, as he grabbed it, and made off hell for leather down Carrick Street, with the whore screaming blue murder as she galloped after him, holding up her loose skirt as she ran.

"'Come back with the friggin loaf,' she kept bawling, but the Hen kept going, knowing well she was handicapped. Just as he was veering to starboard and into the Broomielaw, he heard her giving up the chase as she was fluked, in more ways than one. He also heard her shout something between gasps, something that made him stop dead in his tracks. 'Keep the bloody loaf … You'll need it for a police in the morning,' she screeched.

"I don't know whether he did or not. I don't think so, for I never saw him any the worst by it. No doubt he ate the loaf next day."

"It would take a brave man to face the Carrick Street mob," said Ryan. "It was the only women's model I ever heard of."

"I think there was a book written about it one time," said Tinen.

"There was, and there were room for a few more besides," I added. "Poor old Glasgow was torn asunder by the scribes, yet I never found anything to complain about while there, like every other place, stick your neck out and you get chopped. Mind your own business in Glasgow, and two to one you will be left alone."

Chapter 3

I set Mull and Carney to work in the shaft, and was about to join Tinen on the rakers when McGonagall, the walking pelter, arrived at the pithead, and looked down.

"I see you have put the long fellow down in the hole, Pat," he said aside, but loud enough for Mull to hear. "I only wish it was the right hole as I would enjoy backfilling it." He winked at me.

"Away ye long grass and fish county goat, go back to that hole of a Fermanagh where you came from," roared Mull from below. "See that fellow, Pat?" He pointed a crooked finger up at McGonagall. "I was on the Galloway coast with Carmichael in thirty-seven when that article turned up in his first pair of long trousers, with a snot on him as long as the shovel he was carrying. A shovel that he didn't know what to do with. I think he was looking around for the sweeping brush, thinking the cat had shit under the bed or something. Look at him now, the bee's knees himself. Hitler helped some people."

McGonagall gave a roar of laughter, and wandered away. I joined Tinen. The rest of the gang were on the underpinning, with Young Bob on the Mickey Mouse crane serving both openings.

"Did you see them scaffolders in the canteen this morning, Pat?" Tom said, as he handed me one end of the crosscut saw over the twelve-by-twelve timber on the sawhorse. "There is going to be trouble between that lot yet."

"I agree with you Tom. Dub is sporting a caggy* this morning, and Jock's mouth is cut after yesterday's fracas. They must have been at it again outside the pub. Ah well, when you start something you have to finish it. Were they of our lot they would have shook hands afterwards, and gone their ways without prejudice. I shouldn't wonder but one of them will have an accident shortly."

"No doubt about that but let us get this raker cut before the rain comes or we will get soaked. It's hanging about up there."

We cut and placed the raker in position before the tea break, so the exposed section of piles were now safe. Piles can come forward if unsupported, when rain gets into the ground behind them, and they cannot be shoved back. That's what our job was all about.

The canteen was unusually quiet, in fact there was a reign of silence hanging over the scaffolders' table. The only noisy person was the steam man Dogherty, who was shouting across the room to somebody, loud enough for ganger Murphy's ears, that gangermen were not noted for their card playing. Unemployment cards, yes, as they loved dealing them out. A titter went around in response to this.

Suddenly the peace was shattered by the rattle of rain on the thin roof. It sounded like a thunderstorm. "Send it down Davy," somebody shouted. It lasted for about five minutes before settling down to a steady rhythm.

After a while the walking pelter came in, and ordered everybody out, as the whistle had gone. Nobody moved. Mike Doolan went to the door, looked at the downpour, and remarked, "Sure you wouldn't put an iron gate out in that," then returned to his table, and called for the cards, which appeared like magic. The pelter seeing he was flogging a dead horse, donned an old oilskin he found on the floor, and made a dash for the site office. Anon the rained-off whistle went, to be greeted by a loud cheer.

We were in our usual places around our own table chatting.

"Do you know something," said Mulholland with a shrug. "There is something mighty attractive about that bloody whistle—it's the regalia of authority, something like the Freemason's apron. Every fluken gangerman I've ever met glories in having it. Did you ever watch the bastards blowing it? How they shut their eyes in ecstasy, enjoying it better than a jump."

---

* black eye

"You are damn right Mull," agreed Carney. "I'll tell you about a job I was on at a place called Loch Sloy, up in Scotland. Nuttal was doing the tunnel, and Balfour the dam, which was away up in the mountains, where I worked. The camp being down by the lochside near the Powerhouse site meant that we had to travel to our work daily, by means of an old wartime utility bus. Mind you we were working two twelve-hour shifts, so as one lot came off the other lot went on. All using the same bus. It took about half an hour each way.

"There were two gangers, and a walking pelter among our crowd. The pelter's name was MacKenzie, and the greatest clouster of a man if ever there was one, for he wouldn't make a decent tea boy, the bloody war made him, him being too odd to be shot, more the pity. Now that bus would not wait for you if you were late, no way, so you just lost a shift. Occasionally at was delayed for reasons such as the meal packs being late arriving from the cookhouse, but not very often. You understand there were another crowd waiting to come home. However if we were late, MacKenzie sitting on his usual perch, the front seat, would have his watch in his hand, and dead on seven o'clock blow his whistle, even if we were only halfway up the mountain. In other words, we were under starter's orders there and then. Now what could you make of an idiot with that kind of mentality?"

"Oh, stout," said Tom Tinen, "as thick as broth, sure that's the reason he was there, for no man with any intelligence would have that kind of a job in those days. He was between the ganger and the general, just a dogsbody to do the barking, and a mongrel dog at that."

"Now here's something that is as true as I'm sitting here," I said. "We were down in Aberdare a long time ago on a contract with McAlpine. Aberdare was not a big place then, though no doubt it is now as I haven't been back there since. There were plenty pubs, though.

"Well Saint Patrick's Day it was and we were having a day of it. You must remember those were the days when they celebrated Saint Patrick in style, not like today when most people go to work. Such behaviour in those days would be beyond forgiving. Mac didn't mind atall as it was said he tendered extra to cover Saint Pat's days. I know one thing for sure, nobody would thank you for working. So we were all in the pub, and the landlord highly delighted.

"To put you in the picture regarding Aberdare, the womenfolk didn't like us one bit. You see there weren't much work about the town then, so when McAlpine came in about a lot of the local men went to work for him. Times were hard then, and work when available was hard too. Civil engineering or public works as it was called was harder still. It was proper slavery. The travelling navvy was well used to it up and down the country, but not the poor locals of Aberdare. A few stuck it out, mostly the ex-miners, but a lot could not. They had to jack, but of course to their wives they were fired. Some did ask to be sacked so that they would not lose their dole money, for had they jacked they would be automatically suspended for six weeks. So now you see why the women had a point, and our sympathy.

"However this day was ours, and we were in our element. Drinks flying like there were no tomorrow. Adam's apples bobbing up and down like yo-yos behind dotted neck scarves. The raw whiskey travelling all the way down to the soles of the hobnailed boots, warming hairy shanks under heavy moleskin trousers. 'Here's to Saint Patrick!' somebody shouted, with half a tumbler of whiskey on high.

"There were six women in the pub, seated on a pair of forms that were fixed into the fireside. It was their daily perch, to have their daily physic of a half pint of ale. You could tell that the commotion and noise was annoying them. Furthermore, with all the drinking that was going on around them it seemed to be the only thing going their way. 'Here's to Saint Patrick' came again from somewhere. 'God bless him.'

"'To hell with you and Saint Patrick,' said this sour-looking article on the stool. 'What has he ever done for you? Or for Ireland, come to that.' There was a bit of uncomfortable silence around for a while. Also some deep thinking, as somebody had to give her a smart answer for Saint Patrick's sake.

"'Well,' said this big Mayo gangerman, scratching behind his ear, 'he drove all the snakes out of Ireland.' Somebody shouted 'Hear! Hear!' from a very dark corner.

"'Yes,' said the same woman. 'I think he did, but if he did, he sent them all over here as gangermen for McAlpine.' Was she not the bad owld thing now? Maybe she was right."

"Whether she was or not, she had her answers anyway," said Mull. "I worked with Mac myself for some time. Most of his boss men never left him for to them he was God. Certainly I will admit that he was one of the best to work for, no messing about, and subbed twice a week too. Some of his gangers were a bit thick, though."

"The poor gangerman always gets the thick end of the stick," I said. Some of them are not that bad atall. I've met quite a few good types on my travels up and down the country. I still admit, for every good one you get a bad one."

"Too true," agreed Mull. "We know you are a charge hand timber man, Pat, and that's like being a leading miner on a tunnel face, which is a far cry from being a gangerman. I think half of them know fuckall themselves, but can shout. Those among them civil and good-natured soon become bad through frustration, and ignorance of their work. Them that knows their work can afford to stay good, and do their job manfashion. No shouting and no hassle."

"I don't agree," said Tom Tinen. "The thickness is in them all, and has been since birth, con men most of them. Cripes I knew one who had to get his wife to fill the time sheets for him every night, and got away with it for donkey's years. The subbies' trusted men were the worst of the whole shooting gallery, a pack of pure hounddogs. Listen to this tale about one of them.

"There were a gang of us digging a cable trench along Holloway Road once. A cable trench is not a deep trench as you know. Just about three foot. It was sublet of course and therefore busy. Being on a main street you could only open a certain length at a time, so we were working very close together. One day there came an almighty roar from away back the trench. Apparently a fellow called Big Kilday had unwittingly taken a step backwards, right on top of where Mick Gallagher was working, and in the act of lifting his pick. The howl was Kilday's, as Gallagher's pick got him up the behind, and damn near put him into orbit.

"On hearing the commotion everybody on site ran for the spot. All trying to do something, and nobody doing anything at the same time. However, they did manage to get him out of the trench, and onto a sheet of corrugated iron that was lying by. Whittington Hospital being just up the road, it was decided to take him there as quickly as possible. Therefore away they galloped. Six of them carrying the sheet on which our man was stretched, with the excited gangerman running in front clearing the way, as they had to keep to the road, the footpath being crowded.

"Now there was no truth whatsoever in the story put about the pubs that night by Charlie McFadden, maintaining the ganger was going 'Ahheee … ah-heee … ah-heee' as he ran in front of them. They managed to get him to the hospital at last, but not before they scattered a poor old fellow that was sitting there, waiting for a purgative or something. He would need something right enough after yon mob trampled over him. When the seven angels of mercy reached the casualty section they placed Big Kilday—or what was left of him—on top of the first trolley the saw. Somebody said afterwards that it was a bedpan trolley, but no matter. Then they removed their caps, and stood in a group at his feet, looking as much out of place as seven priests would, standing in Madame Tussaud's Chamber of Horrors.

"The duty sister espied them, how in the hell wouldn't she. So like a dreadnought she charged towards them. A tough-looking cookie of the no-nonsense variety. She looked at the man stretched on the corrugated sheet on top o' the trolley. He was lying facedown, chin resting on one forearm, eyes staring straight ahead, and as white as a ghost. His cap, which he still held firmly by the peak, covered the spot where the damage was done. 'What's wrong with him?' she demanded.

"The owld gangerman looked at her in a kind of disbelief—as he was never inside a hospital in his life she surely surprised him by having to ask. He assumed that people in hospitals knew their business without having to ask questions. He never had to ask any questions when at work, because he knew his stuff. 'He got a pick up his arse,' said he, wiping his big red nose with his cap.

"The dragon lifted all her chins, and lowered her eyebrows, then stared down her long nose at him, as if he was some kind of a germ who got into her sterilised temple. 'Don't be so vulgar,' she snapped. 'Rectum.'

"The owld ganger had about enough of her. 'Wrecked him?' he said. 'You bloody idjit, it fucking near killed him.'

"Needless to say the whole bunch of them were chased from the premises, except Kilday, who was wheeled away to be darned where it hurt.

"After an hour or two he arrived back on site to collect his bits and pieces. By now the large subbie was there himself, talking away to the gangerman out of the corner of his mouth. The ganger noticing Kilday, turned round and asked how he was, more out of shame than sympathy. The subbie said nothing, just stood there.

"'Oh, I'm not bad. The doctor wanted me to stay in for the night, which was very kind of him, but I refused, as he has enough on his plate. So he told me to take some pills with some slimy oil he gave me, and to stay off work for a week.'

"The subbie looked at him in amazement. 'Stay off work! Stay off work, sure it's your feet you work with,' he growled.

"What do you make of that lot now?"

"Ach. Tinen, you are enough to drive anybody to drink," I laughed.

"But it's true, Pat. I was there, and furthermore, at a later date when some distance further on, somebody dropped a dirty big sleeper down a newly dug manhole, and hit this fellow in the back. It felled him like a strucken ox. They took him to the same hospital, and the gangerman went into the casualty department to tell the duty sister that he had a badly injured man outside. 'What's wrong with him?' she asked. 'I think his back is broken.' 'I better have a look at him then.'

"So she followed him out, to where a JCB digger was parked at the foot of the entrance steps, and there stretched in the front bucket was the patient, more dead than alive. The sister let out a screech. 'Holy cripes!' she exclaimed. 'If it wasn't broken when you left, it's bloody well broken now. How far have you brought him?' 'Just about two miles,' proudly answered the gangerman come ambulance man. Just imagine taking the poor man all that way in the bouncing bucket of a JCB."

"I've seen a kerbstone snap in one of them buckets," said Ryan, "and that poor bugger's back was half-cracked already."

"Come on boys it's opening time," said Mull, as he made for the door. There will be a better crack in the Hog, for this rain is on for the duration.* So once more we were gathered in the Hog ordering beer and listening to the landlord's complaints about the weather, you would think it was him who was rained off.

We were the same gang as Monday's but with the addition of Charlie Ryan and the exclusion of Malone. Ryan, no way related to Whispering Mick, was working on a job nearby. He was a sidekick of Mull's, and

---

* a wartime expression

as sure as hell where one showed up the other followed, yet they never seemed to agree.

Ryan was a Cork man about the same age as Mull though he looked older.

Mull reckoned he was about ninety. He was a first-class timber man. "Here's cheers," said Mull, as he raised his glass. "Without a doubt the first pint is the best," he added, licking his lips, before wiping them with the back of his hand.

"Ryan," he said, "on your creeping about the country dodging the column, did you ever come across Big MacCutchen. A Scot. The reason I am asking is that I overheard him saying once that a certain Ryan owed him a few pounds. Of course had he asked me I would have denied any knowledge of you, and told him that people owing money were not in my circle of friends."

"Circle of friends be buggered," roared Ryan, "you two-faced hound-dog. Why don't you get back and repay that fiver you owe the landlord of the Balmoral in Hawick, and that's over five years ago."

"Hold the line there Ryan, one never owes a landlord anything. It is illegal for the publican to lend you money for drink, so anything he gives you is just a rebate, nothing more. When the tax man gives you a rebate you don't owe it to him or give it back. Not atall. A rebate is a rebate."

"Well," said Ryan, "rebate or loan, or what else you choose to call, it I don't owe Big Mac anything. Anyway, if I did he would be the last man to mention it. As for knowing him, we worked together for a very long time."

"OK, OK," said Mull, waving his hand, "keep your shirt on I was only joking, and I was well aware of you knowing him."

"Who was MacCutchen?" asked Young Bob. Along with being inquisitive he knew well that a name mentioned would have a tale attached.

"Oh. A bit of a character, Bob," I said, "more than likely retired by now."

"That he was," added Mull. "One of the finest men to come out of Scotland. Six foot three in his stocking soles, as broad as a door, and with a mop of red thatch over a freckled face that carried a built-in smile. Could fight like a rooster, and work like a mule. He was a good singer too when he had a few jars. 'The Wild Colonial Boy' was his favourite song."

"I'll tell you something you didn't know about him," said Ryan. "His people were travellers, and so was he in his early years. He once told me that he was born by the roadside near Carlisle, which makes him English, though he always maintained to be Scottish. His father and mother were, and it was by dint of pure accident that he decided to make his appearance where he did, on the roadside, on a market day in Carlisle. You see, his people were holed up on a piece of waste ground at Gretna—where they marry in a hurry—and his mother had gone into Carlisle to hawk some odds and sods, which was part and parcel of their living. She was on her way home again when the young Mac made up his mind that enough was enough, and decided to make his move. So realising that the young rip was going to pull freight, she made for the shelter of a wee bank by the roadside, where she would be hidden from passing eyes. By good luck she was carrying a brand-new galvanised bucket she bought in town. So there and then—or so he said himself—he was shot into the bucket. Then wrapped in an old cardigan, and thus carried home. It never done him any hard, though, for he grew up a fine strapping man.

"Some years later as a young man he immigrated to Australia, where he spent most of his time in the great outback, doing all sorts of work, sheep shearing included. By the way, never let him cut your hair for I seen a bloke that did. Well you couldn't help seeing him for he was simply scalped. He also worked on the Snowy Mountains hydro scheme while there, knocking about the camps, which were pretty rough I believe.

"Eventually he came home to his native Scotland, married a nice Australian girl he met in Dundee, and they took to the road together, while he still followed the navvying game. She was not of the travelling stock, but sure them outback Aussies are a 'Waltzing Matilda' sort of travellers themselves.

"After a few years a pair of boys appeared on the scene. A nice little family to settle down with, which they did, after managing to get a wee council house in a village outside Perth.

However Mac's problems were far from over as the villagers didn't take to them, being travellers. But their greatest bugbear was the young ones, who had picked up some choice words during their sojourn on the roads. Words most of the neighbours had never heard before, especially their youngsters. The one good thing about it was, that the pair had also picked up their parent's Australian drawl, which bamboozled the neighbours so much, they just couldn't understand them. Mac was well aware of this, and knew full well it was only a matter of time before somebody cottoned on. Then the fat could be in the fire. If enough complained they might lose the house. So in desperation he went to see an Irish doctor that practiced in Perth. To seek his advice. 'How old are they?' asked the doctor. 'Five and four. We have tried everything on them, soap in their mouths which didn't help, locked them in a dark cupboard under the stairs which made them worse, even I was educated. We just don't know what to do, doctor.' 'My advice to you,' said the medicine man, 'is to go back to the old ways, which is, to give them a damn good clout below the ear every time they swear, and make sure it's constant.'

"The following morning being Sunday, Mac was up bright and early to put the doctor's prescription to the test. So he stood at the bottom of the stairs and called them down for breakfast. When they came, the eldest first, Mac asked him, 'What do ye want fer breakfast?' 'I'll have fucking cornflakes,' he replied.

"Mac made a hoop of him under the stairs, with a wallop. Then he turned to the four-year-old who was now halfway down the stairs, and asked him what he wanted. The young buck looked at his mate sitting on the floor blubbering, then replied, very seriously, 'Christ! I'd be a cunt if I asked for cornflakes.' It was Mac himself that told me about that, when we worked together."

When the laughing ceased, I managed to add, "They were a chip of the old block for I also worked with the man, long ago. It was on a rock tunnel job in Glen Affric. He was a powerful fit man, sure after finishing his shift he was fresher than some of the men going on."

"I have never ventured into the tunnels," said Ryan. "I'm a bit big for that work I think. So I left it to the broadset Donegalmen."

"Too big!" said Mull. "Too fucking lazy would be more to the point."

"It must be rough work in the rock tunnels," commented Bob.

"Oh, it's rough sure enough," answered Mull. "They don't link them as they go like soft ground tunnels, not until they drive in through. Just the bare jaggy rock overhead, with water pissing down on you continuously. You wear a helmet, oilskin jacket, and rubber boots as protective clothing. The oilskin trousers you couldn't wear, as they made you sweat too much. Needless to say with ripping and tearing amount the drills and rock, you were soaked from start to finish of the shift. Good for the bones in latter days."

"It gave some old bastards something to boast about too," chipped in Tinen.

"Damn that for a game," said Bob. "You can stick it as far as I'm concerned, no doubt the camps were just as bad."

"Indeed they were," I said. "Some of the hardest men walking were gathered in those camps. The fit and the dying, the thief and the con man, some that didn't work atall but lived on their wits. All arguments were settled behind the wet-canteen, and if you were not man enough to do so you had better pull freight. A handshake afterwards, and a good drink left no hard feelings."

"Talking about camps," said Ginger, "reminds me of a tale I heard when working in a place called Dalcroy. That was the name of the camp. Being a hydro contract it was as usual stuck away up on the moors, miles from anywhere. In fact the nearest town was Pitlochry, and that were eight miles away. There were more than a thousand men in that camp, and like all such places the goings and comings were frequent. Especially at weekends. This story is about a pair of lads that had jacked on the Friday, and with the best intentions in the world meant to be on the bus to town that evening. Well as they say, the best laid plans … They didn't. Having met a new arrival whom they knew of old, the night passed in drinking each other's health, and so did Saturday. Sunday being a dead day with no transport anywhere, was spent in camp, where a bottle or two could always be got providing you had the funds.

"Monday morning finds the two tramping the road to Pitlochry, one on each side of the road—as if they couldn't bear each other's company— silent and skint. Suddenly one of them stopped in his tracks, with a pensive look on his face. His mate also stopped, to give him a querying look. 'You know something Charlie?' he muttered. 'We are flat broke. Skint, kaput! Therefore drastic needs force drastic measure. Right?' Charlie shrugged in collaboration.

"'Right then, there is always a jock or two jacks every Monday morning, unable to face the music. Now as there is no transport until midday there ought to be one of them along anytime now, so we hide in the ditch, and roll the first one along. What do you say?' 'Drastic sure enough,' said Charlie, 'but needs must, as you said.'

"So in behind a big whin bush, in a dry ditch lay the pair of ambushers. Charlie maintaining he could tell a Glaswegian's footsteps a mile away as they walked faster than other.

"Sure enough after a while along came a victim, and apparently in a fierce hurry, for he didn't see the villains until too late when they were upon him. Man alive there was one almighty scrap! It took them a long time before they managed to floor him, and rifle his pockets. One hell of a skirmish altogether. However the Glaswegian eventually managed to break loose, and make off like a hare, leaving the pair sitting in the middle of the road licking their wounds, and they had plenty of them. Charlie now with no sleeve in his coat, and a black eye coming up, asked, 'How much did he have on him?' 'Fluking hell, only seven and six,' said his mate in disgust as he nursed his ear, which was half hanging off, and rubbed a grazed knee through torn trousers. 'Cripes!' said Charlie. 'We're bloody lucky—if he had a pound on him, he would have killed the fucking pair of us.'"

Amid the laughter around me, I was thinking to myself that most people would pass that yarn off as a joke, but they could be wrong. I would not like to say how authentic that story is, but knowing the times and place I do not doubt but something of the sort took place. I could vouch for dafter tricks that that.

"I suppose they were a pair of Donegal men," I heard Mulholland say out of the corner of his mouth, grinning, and nodded in my direction.

"Piss off back to Geordieland," I said, "and join the rest of your clique sleeping against Hadrian's Wall, waiting for somebody to wake you with a cry, 'To the wall! To the wall!' Only nowadays it's not the Scots that are coming to rob your cattle, but probably the shilling-a-week tallyman, or it's opening time."

"Well you must admit there were a mighty lot of Donegal men around Scotland then, it being the nearest jumping-off point. Also there was more rock in Scotland than in England, to keep them busy. Sure the Long Dogherty, himself a Donegalman, used to say: 'If you throw a stone into a whin bush in Scotland, if it is not a rabbit that comes out of it, it's bound to be a Donegalman.' He should know, having tramped enough of it in his time."

"There were quite a few Mayo men about it too," I replied.

"The Dogherty was some flower," mused Mull. "A great dragliner when he decided to be so, it was said that he could pick up an egg at a distance of fifty feet with the bucket, without breaking it."

"Could have done with eating it, instead of fluking about with it the long slug," said Tinen. "I had to laugh at him one night in this pub. As you know he was always in some kind of jeopardy, never getting things quite right, be it a statement or an argument. He was drinking along with this Mayman, a driver of some sort no doubt. Anyway when he asked Dogherty where he came from, he was told: 'Where they plant the cabbages with a jackhammer.' 'Huh!' said Mayo. 'Not bad atall. Down my way, I once seen a man planting carrots with a mallet.'"

There was some spluttering into beer mugs at that crack.

Four men from a neighbouring site now joined Ned Corrigan and his mate at an adjacent table. Among them was Taffy the banksman, who was the life and soul of any gathering. He took some stick regarding his native Wales, but gave better in return. Old Ned was a ganger on the same site, so no doubt Taff had made a beeline for him to get him going.

"What's wrong with the Crown today," someone asked.

"Too bloody crowded," answered Taff.

"It always is at the end of the month," remarked Tinen. "Office workers get paid by the month so they are all millionaires today. It will be back to the luncheon voucher and the half pint again tomorrow. Still they were here before us, and will be after we are gone."

"I suppose you are right, Tom," sighed Taff.

We all tuned in to our own company once more. "I laughed at that yarn about the two boyos and their attempt at rolling the Glaswegian," chuckled Magehie. "Some clowns are daft enough for anything."

"Oh, indeed they were," agreed Ginger, "especially in that camp anyway. Were you ever there?"

"No, I was never in any of them, though I've heard about them right enough, and what I heard wasn't good. Still, no matter how bad things are one can always find a funny side to it. Just like war."

"Too true," I agreed. "Now that you bring it to mind, I'll tell you about a funny thing that happened, up there.

"We were in this camp situated a few miles North of Blair Atholl in Perthshire. It was called Calvine, after a little hamlet nearby. It was built early in the war, to house internees. Mostly Italians as their country was at war with Britain. So being internees and not prisoners of war they were well treated, and so they should. The camp was well laid out, and well cared for by the occupants, for they bore no grudge. When the war ended and contractors moved in to use it as a labour camp for their hydro schemes, its respectability died. Don't blame the contractors, leave that to the objects they installed there as worksmen. They came from all walks of life, and in my opinion, some came out from under flat stones. There were English, Irish, Scots, Welsh, Poles, ex German prisoners of war, and a basketful of Europeans allsorts. It was a proper hell's stewpot, with drinking, fighting, and gambling. You name the game, and it was played there. The crown and anchor was the main one, and there were three boards in operation. One in particular was operating in the camp square, what used to be a beautiful marble altar, built by the Catholic Italians to celebrate open-air Mass, was now used as a gambling table by a Catholic Irishman for his crown-and-anchor board. A bit ironic eh! Who knows, perhaps it might still be consecrated ground.

"In the huts, some men slept in their clothes, including their willies. Too drunk to do otherwise. Others were sick on the bare floorboards. It was a godsend they were bare with wide gaps between them—as they were warped—which relieved some of the stink. They only means of heating was a round letterbox stove that stood in the centre of the hut. It burned coke. In some huts it was half buried by a ring of ashes, crowned with a selection of sweaty socks and toerags.

"Now and again when the canteen was closed, somebody in a half-drunken state would bring forth a tin kettle, and decide to brew up. Then produce a loaf with a pot of jam, and commence to smother large doorstep slices with it, using his bed as a table. Most of the jam went on the blanket.

"There was supposed to be a hut orderly for every four huts to keep them clean, but as people were on alternate shifts and the beds were in constant use, any orderly unable to dodge a flying boot kept out of the way, and let them get on with it. Some huts in certain areas were neat, and well kept.

"Most of the orderlies and canteen cleaners were city winos who were only there for their grub and beg, plus what they could scrounge. For instance, the crown and anchor barons never allowed small change on their boards, so should anyone lay a bet in small silver, the operator would pick it up, put it in his coat pocket, and replace it with its nearest value in two-bob bits, or half crowns. Always overvalued though. Such was their law. At the end of the night's gambling they would empty their coat pockets on to the board, and toss it all up in the air. That was the start pistol for the melee royal among the orderlies and cleaners, as they fought tooth and nail for the loose money, on their hands and knees, pulling and tugging at each other like a lot of scavenging vultures. They came from all corners of the damp to hover round the outskirts of the gamblers near the close of play, waiting to dive on the money. Needless to say as they scrambled among the forest of legs, the gamblers' main sport was leaping about to see how many hands they could tramp on with two feet. A good job most of them wore wellies. Now that's man's inhumanity to man, as Rabbie Burns said.

"Our hut was number thirty, a better type of hut, and one of four situated at the back of the camp. It was occupied by a good bunch of lads, who made sure the orderly did his duty whether there were men asleep or not. They did bribe him a bit, though, with an odd bottle of beer and such. It was one of the few huts an orderly could take the camp boss to inspect, in order to justify his existence. There weren't many such.

"There were twenty-four men in each hut. Twelve on each side, with a tall locker by each bed. They could be quite comfortable, you know.

"A fellow by name of Sean Boyle was next to me at the far end of the hut. All the occupants, with the exception of one, were on the same shift, which made life easier. The exception was an old ex-gangerman by the name of Mick Flood. He was long since retired, and stayed with his sister in Glasgow, but like a lot of old-timers, when the weather improved he awoke from his hibernation, and made for the Highland camps. Knowing that the men in charge would fix him up with a light job—of which there were plenty about—for the summer.

"Mick was working on the tip, cleaning skips and greasing axles. He was a nice old devil, except for one damnable habit that affected us to a man, especially when on dayshift. You see, every night he would take himself to the wet-canteen and guzzle beer until closing time, then return to the hut loaded, but never drunk. The problem: He had a weak bladder, and rose for a piss practically every hour during the night. As the toilet's some distance away, he commandeered a large seven-pound jam tin he found behind the cookhouse, and kept it under his bed as a pot. That was fair enough had he used it properly, but no. He persisted, or so it seemed, to hold it at arm length and let rip. The rattle he made, accompanied by grunts and farts, was far beyond a joke, especially to men who had just finished a hard twelve-hour shift. He was roared at constantly, but it made no difference.

"We often discussed it in his absence, and wondered what could be done about it seeing as he would not take a telling. Then one fine evening when we're all lying on top of our beds cracking about this and that, the subject of Mick and his pisspot came up. Sean Boyle—who was a bit of a rascal anyway—suddenly jumped from his bed and pulled on his boots saying, 'I'll fix the bugger good and proper,' as he made out the door. He returned a while later carrying a large tin of health salts, pulled Mick's tin from under the bed, made sure it was dry before he emptied to whole dollop into it, then pushed it back under the bed. 'That will fix him,' he said, grinning.

"We were all bedded down when Mick came in. He went through his usual rigmarole of shedding his skins, of which he had more than an onion. We were all feigning sleep, and waiting. It was about an hour afterwards when we heard the tin being toed along the floor. The bladder was calling. Now my friends, water on liver salts is lively enough stuff, but you just imagine hot piss on a whole tinful. Jases man! It erupted like a volcano. The foam rose with such a hiss, it was like the safety valve of a steam engine blowing off, though it was nearly drowned by the roars of Mick.

"'Holy japers! I'm fucked! I'm done for! I'm croaked! Them damn gallstones have burst! Burst as sure as there is balls in a cat! That bloody doctor in Glasgow told me, there were so many of them, he could quarry them at a profit, said he would do away with them. Damn him anyway. The only remedy for stones is blasting. He must have given me something to make them explode—now they have, just like firing the face. Holy japers! I'm destroyed. I'm a dead duck, fucked by a rake of bloody gallstones.'

"All this time he was dancing around the floor in his long johns, though no longer visible under a shirt of sparkling froth, and still holding on to the foaming caldron. No one could do anything, being paralysed with laughter. Eventually I managed to take the champagne tin from him, and slung it out the door, where it lay on its side still bubbling. It took a lot of effort to get him back to bed again, where he sat up all night, taking an odd peep under the clothes to make sure things didn't start off again.

"In the morning he was up with the lark, and fully dressed when we stirred. His bag was packed ready for Glasgow, and his doctor. That was the last we saw of him. We heard he came back after a week to another camp further up the glen."

"Ach! Sure them old fellows being as healthy as frogs all their lives, couldn't understand things going wrong, with age. They didn't know what illness was," said Ginger. "Charlie McFadden was telling me about an old boy that he knew who was retired, and inquisitive through boredom. Apparently a doctor attending a neighbour one day was stopped and questioned by him as he passed his door. True enough, doctors' visits were a rarity in them days, too bloody dear. The doctor told him it was just a confinement case. 'Cripes,' said he, 'that's serious enough. I nearly died from that one year myself, doctor.' So you see what he knew about illness."

A large ginger-haired fellow at the bar was singing an old Irish ballad. He could sing too.

At the next table Taffy was arguing with ganger Ned. A pair of clowns together if ever there were two, for we knew them of old.

Ned was saying, "You must of off your rocker, Taff, if you believe that every time an express train hits a midge, it has to stop. Such things might happen in Wales, but nowhere else. What do you say lads?" he asked, as he turned to our table looking for support. "This man is mad."

"I wouldn't be knowing anything about trains," said Mull. "It's thirty years since I was on one, and that one stopped fairly often being the narrow gauge type. Whether it stopped for midges or people, I didn't ask the driver. You better be a bit more explicit Taff."

"Look here man," said Taff, turning to face Mull, "I'm just trying to tell this thickhead of a gangerman something he can't fathom." He now turned back to face Ned. "Give me your watch for a minute, Ned," he asked. Ned reluctantly unhooked the watch from his waistcoat buttonhole, and handed it to him.

"Right," said Taff, as be placed his elbows on the table, and held the watch by the chainbar, letting it swing to and fro. "Look by here now at this watch, as it swings backward and forward like the pendulum of a clock. It stands to reason, man, that it has to stop at the end of its swing, before it can turn back."

"I suppose so," agreed Ned after a while.

"Bloody hell man, there is no supposed about it," said the vexed Taff.

"If you push a bogie into a bleeding tunnel, you have to stop it before you can push it out again. Be reasonable man."

A few of the listeners nodded in agreement with that. Ned included, but hesitant, being aware of his standing as a ganger he couldn't afford to slip up.

"Right," continued Taffy, giving Ned back his watch, his point proven.

"Now we have a bumbee flying along between a pair of railway tracks, minding its own business you could say, when along comes an express train going like the clappers, and flattens him. The bumbee is now squashed right against the engine, and stopped in relations to the ground. He has to be before he can return on his track. Therefore the bloody engine must be stopped! Common sense man—one can't be stopped and the other moving when they are solid together."

We all pondered on this for a spell. Then the 'Kingfisher and Leader of Men', Ned himself, shouted out: "I've got it." He never heard of the eureka bit. "What happens is the same thing that happens when you get clouted by something, it splits you open, only with the bumbee it's a more serious matter. He is split from arsehole to breakfast time, after being hit with a blooming big engine. He is split right down the middle you see, with each half going different ways, like east and west making two half circles, so the movement is continuous. In fact he turns around within himself just like two people dancing, he doesn't stop at all."

"Holy hell! What a load of crap!" cried Taffy in despair as he held his head and turned his back on Ned in disgust. After a minute he turned again. "You bloody idiot you." He shook his head. "If what you say is right every damn bumbee you see on the front of an engine must be turned inside out. Have a look the next time you are at a station, and watch out, don't tell them what you are looking for, or they will surely send for the men in the white coats."

Ned was now scratching his head in confusion, while the rest laughed their heads off.

"There must be some way out of it," he muttered sheepishly.

"Of course there is, Ned," answered Tinen. "You see the turning of the bumble bee takes place in the cushion of air that is pushed in front of the engine, and he is already on his way back before the engine catches up with him. Hence the reason why there is not a mark on his corpse when you see it stuck on the front of an engine or the radiator of a car."

"Perhaps Ned's argument would hold water," said Mull, "if the bumbee was a kind of ganger bumbee—then you wouldn't notice if he was inside out or outside in, just the same as a big stone you split with a hammer, or one of them concrete test cubes the engineers keep squashing to smithereens."

Everyone laughed except Ned.

"Sure, it's like that old question, if you jump off a wall, where were you when you jumped?" remarked Young Bob.

"On the wall, surely," answered Tinen.

"No, that was before you jumped, and don't say in the air, for that was after you jumped."

"Ach, balls!" somebody muttered.

"Isn't it wonderful the mighty intelligence you find around a public house table on a damp day," remarked Mull.

"I remember a character once by the name of MacKinnoch," I said. "I suppose he is dead by now. He would amaze you with his card tricks in the pub. He was hot stuff, yet nobody ever seen him play a game. A good job too for he would skog the bloody lot. He would stand before the dartboard, and mesmerise you with his sleight of hand, old and knobbly as they were the dexterity of them was something worth seeing. He must have been on the stage at some time."

"If he was, it was staging muck down in a hole he was," said Ginger. "He was sharp I'll admit, but the reason why he stood in front of the dartboard was so that nobody could see what he was doing behind what he appeared to be doing. He was never theatre-class, though."

"Well I wouldn't know, as I have never stood in a theatre in my life," muttered Mull.

"What is Taffy up to now?" somebody asked.

"Ach! He is always at some devious capers," replied Ginger, looking over his shoulder. "Match tricks no doubt, as he is good at them."

"Talking about matches," said Ryan, who up to now had been fairly quiet, "I'll show you timber men a thing you never seen before. Tom, you have just bought a box of matches—can I see it?" Tom brought forth the box. "Now, will you tip them out on the table in a heap, and hand me the empty box." After he got the box, he examined it thoroughly before opening it and placing it on the table. Then he selected three matches from the heap, measured them methodically against the width of the box, and broke them off to the exact fit before carefully fixing them at equal spacing, in and across the box. After a final examination he gently closed the box, and placed it side-up in the centre of the table. A crowd of onlookers had now gathered from surrounding tables. All eyes on the mysterious box. "Now mister," Ryan addressed Tinen, "I'll bet you that you will not harm that box, no matter how hard you hit it. As a timber man, you have seen and understand how well shored it is inside."

There was a moment of silence, as everyone was looking from Ryan to Tinen, then back to the box.

"Ach! Fluking fiddlesticks," roared Tinen, as he brought a mighty fist down on the box with a thump that shook every pint on the table. It even made the landlord look our way. Needless to say the matchbox—made of wood shavings—was in smithereens, plastered to the table. Everybody was now staring at Ryan. Tinen was leaning back with a broad grin on his old weather-beaten face.

"Now then," said Ryan so cool and calm, as he lit his pipe, then pointed a dirty ash-stained finger at the heap of matches on the table and asked, "what are you going to do with this little lot then?"

As Tinen stared at the heap, an almighty roar of laughter bust from around the table. Tinen with a face that would do credit to a Red Indian statue, just sat there dumbfounded, staring at the heap. Then with a rueful smile he swiped the lot clear of the table, with the back of his hand. "Ach! Bugger you, Ryan," he said. "I'll get you yet."

Young Bob shaking with laughter and drying his eyes with the corner of his donkey jacket, shoved his chair back as he got up, saying, "I'm going to catch some client at the bar with that," and he made off. I could see a lot of matches lying around before the day was out.

"Hoy Bob," Ginger called after him, "keep away from ganger Murphy. Dogherty might have upset him again at the cards. Wait till you get home and try it on your landlord—his wife's large kitchen box should make a decent pile."

"If he does, he will be looking for a new pad tomorrow," I added, "as it is, he might earn himself a thick ear from Murphy."

Well, they say. You can't age the young, and sure enough within minutes there came a great roar of laughter from the bar, accompanied by a howl of rage. Then from the crowd broke the grinning Bob, making hell for leather for the door, with Murphy hard on his heels, clutching a large handful of matches.

"Be japers if he gets a hold of him, he will skin him alive," said Ginger, shaking his head.

It was a while before the door flew open again, and the pair came back in, the grinning Murphy leading Bob by the ear, with his head dripping wet. Murphy had shoved it under a full running gutter at the corner of the house.

"That will larn ye," grinned Mull, as we watched Bob return to his seat and make an effort to dry his hair with the corner of his donkey coat, still grinning from ear to ear. Apparently it was all worth it. I noticed Tinen was also smiling, as he was no longer alone.

A big pint was shoved in front of Bob from behind his back. "Here ye young rip," came with it. It was Murphy.

"By gum they must be clearing out Camden Town with yon lot is coming here," said Mull, as he nodded towards the door. We all looked in that direction, to see the well-known face of Big John Brogan making for the bar, with a gusto that would do credit to an arid Arab, making for an oasis. He took his pint and as he turned and took a slug, his eyes went rubbering about the room, until we fell in the way of his wandering gaze. There was no piano!

He came towards us, nodding to an acquaintance here and there on his way. On reaching our table he just placed his tumbler on it, then turned to address Taff's table.

"You fellows don't seem to mind who you sit next to, do you. Surely you could pick better neighbours."

"Ach!" said Taffy. "Beggars can't be choosy, and they don't smell."

"Sit down you fluking idjit," said Mull, as he pulled in a chair. "You make a decent place untidy. So you do. I suppose they threw you out of Camden Town for buying too much drink."

Brogan sat, nodding to all around. "If I was buying, it was with my own money I was buying, and nobody else's." He turned to me. "How are things, Pat? Where did you get a hold of this article?" He jerked his thumb over his shoulder towards Mulholland. "The last I heard of him, he was rooting a hole down about Southampton. God knows what shape it was in after he left, it would be neither square nor round. Are you all across the road?"

"Yep," I answered. "It's not a bad setup. I suppose, as good as what's going. Where have you hailed from, as you haven't been around for quite a while."

"More than likely after coming out of clink, if you ask me," chipped in Mull. "Out early in the mornings stealing some poor baby's milk from some secluded doorstep. I'll warrant you. The same man would steal a mouse from a blind kitten."

Brogan was Glasgow Irish, but like a lot of navvies he had no accent. He was another long-distance man, and an old road mate of Mull's. They were about the same age. No one ever heard a civil word pass between him, Mull, or Ryan, who was quieter than usual today. I suppose it was just their way of going on.

"I have just pulled out of Stockton-on-Tees, Pat," he answered, ignoring Mull. "I left there yesterday, no good." Then he noticed Tinen for the first time, seated between me and the wall, and saluted in his direction. "I should have known that the secretary wouldn't be far away! There were a few around there you would know, by the way—do you remember the Slinger? Well he's dead, died in Scunthorpe, where he lived for quite a few years in retirement. Good crack he was in his day."

"Indeed and he was that," I agreed. "Must have been in his late seventies."

"He would be," nodded Mull. "He certainly was a bit of a lad alright. I remember him telling about a time he had to go and see this subbie, about some work. It was a building site, and the subbie needed a drainlayer. The Slinger never liked subbies, and liked small building sites less. However needs must when the devil drives, you might say. So he went to see the man, who was a very busy little man by what I've heard. Right away he took Slinger round the place to show him what he wanted.

"'You start here,' said he. 'There you cut to pick up that manhole, after that you carry on, but cut again to pick up this sink pipe. When you come near to that second manhole you have to cut and—' 'Hold the fluking line there,' roared Slinger. 'It's a bloody tailor you need,' and he made off."

"Oh, he was cranky without a doubt," I agreed. "Especially where young gangers were concerned. He didn't like them, reckoning as they were too frightened to steal, too lazy to work, so they became gangers. He said the same about subbies, who he held in the same esteem."

"He could have been right," said Tinen. "Who the hell likes subbies anyway! In his day they were worse, if such a thing could be possible. Thanks God most of them bad things are all gone now, the younger generation won't wear them. The cable-laying bastards were the worst. Not only did they break a man's back digging, but they made him pull the blinking cable along the trench afterwards. Imagine twenty men spaced about two yards apart, and tugging at a big cable as thick as your leg, to the 'Heave' calls of the timing gangerman. Too stout to use a winch, maintaining they couldn't use one, as they might damage the armour-coated cable. Balderdash! They got more money for hand hauling—that was the prime reason. Later on, when the price differences disappeared, by cripes they weren't long in getting a winch on the job then."

"Damn right," agreed Brogan. "But what annoyed me was hearing some gabshites in the pubs, boasting about how they pulled this cable and that cable, for this subbie and that subbie, and bleeding proud of it too. They were worse than the subbie. Most of them couldn't pull a nail, but listen. I heard a story about a fluker I once worked for, by the name of Breen.

"He was finishing off a job in Saint Albans, a cable job of course. It was on the Friday, and he turned up himself to make sure everything was in order, and to pay off the men. Which he did, with the exception of a pair of clowns he called to one side, telling them to be back there on Monday morning, to tidy up, and that he would meet them there.

"Right enough they were there, and so was the bold subbie, who told one of them to jump into the car so he could take him up the road and show him a little job that needed doing. He showed him the job alright, and explained what he wanted done. Then on their way back he explained some more. 'Listen,' he said. 'I'm getting rid of that other clouster this evening, as he is no good. I have another big job starting tomorrow, and

I want you on it, but first, you must make sure everything is finished here by tonight. Make sure of that by keeping that bugger working. So here is his money, but don't give it to him until the evening, when everything is done. OK?'

"'Sound,' yelped our man as he leapt out of the car, with a rough shake of his shoulders, and a thumb up in the air. 'You can count on me.' He grabbed his shovel, and to show willing made off at a gallop up the road, shovel held in both hands, ready to move mountains.

"When the subbie seen him out of sight, he called the other idjit to him. What do you know! Didn't he tell him the exact same tale he was after telling his so-called mate, giving him his money an all. Then well satisfied with his morning's work he drove off, no doubt grinning from ear to ear.

"Now was that not a damnable trick to play on a pair of galoots. Imagine the pair of them slaving away all day to get the job finished, while throwing a sly look towards each other, smirking to themselves in a kind of 'I know something you don't know!' attitude. Then in the evening, standing there with each other's money in their hands. From what I heard, they knocked fluke out of each other. What else could they do! Pure embarrassment no doubt, didn't they deserve all they got for being so thick."

"By japers," I said. "That was a dirty one sure enough. But damn them, too, good for them. I know what I would give a subbie, were he to suggest such a thing. A good kick up the hole."

"Damn right," agreed Ginger.

"You know they are not all bad," said Mull with a smile. "Some can have a good laugh at themselves, no doubt that subbie did!"

"Well gents," I said, picking up my pot. "The crack is over for another day. I don't think any of you hear the bell as we are practically the only ones left, so there's cheers."

"I see what you mean," said Mull, looking round. "Anybody going my way?"

"I am," said Ginger, rising. "See you all tomorrow."

"Hold the line a bit, Mulholland," said Brogan. "I better come along with you as far as Camden Town."

"Cripes! That's all I need. Are you afraid of getting lost? Here, hold my hand."

"Piss off."

As I passed the site the gates were still open, as there was a lowloader in the entrance unloading another dragline machine, plus a pair of pumps. The pumps would be sorely needed by the amount of water lying on site.

Ach well! That was tomorrow's problem.

Chapter 4

We started work at eight o'clock, and most of the morning was spent on pumping and bailing out holes. The only dry spot was Mulholland's shaft, as the existing segment shaft had acted as a soak-away.

"How are things?" asked the pelter McGonagall at my elbow.

"OK for now, but there were eight foot of water in both holes, which won't do the timber much good! Tight as a drum."

"Aye. I can see that bottom whaler is bending a bit. You will need an extra strut there, Pat."

"Yep. I'll try and shove it back with a trench prop first, but nobody is going down there for a while after that. Need to give the place a chance to dry out. That's if the rain keeps off."

"We'll be lucky," he replied, looking up at the sky and slushing off through the mud.

He was right, for shortly afterwards the sky opened up, to send us racing for the canteen.

"I think we should build a bloody ark instead of a post office," shouted McGonagall as he galloped past, making for the office.

By the time breakfast was over and the chiefs had received the forecast, the rained-off whistle went. So it being just about opening time the men drifted away in pairs, until there were only a handful of teetotallers left to study their papers in peace.

The pub was crowded when Tinen and I arrived, but somebody had two pints waiting for us.

"Where is Magehie going, does anybody know?" asked Ginger. "I seen him collect his cards this morning."

"I think he is heading for Carlisle," I replied. "There's a rock-tunnel job going on there, no doubt trying to get his head under for the winter."

"Talking about Magehie, and rock tunnels," said Ryan, "is it not strange that we are sitting here rained off because of a drop of water, yet that man is going to work in a daily downpour of the bloody stuff, what's the difference! We are stopped from working, but rock miners carry on."

"God save us," answered Tinen. "If you were waiting for it to stop raining in a rock tunnel, it would never be driven. Different environment altogether—you get paid for the conditions you expect in a rock job."

"I suppose you are right," sighed Ryan. "Tunnel work is strange work indeed, and so are the buggers who follow it. They all seem know each other, and stick together like glue to a blanket, you never hear of any young blood among them."

"Oh, I don't know about that," I said. "Young ones have to start somewhere. They are there, but you don't hear about them until they are established. They gradually slip in as the older ones move out."

"Every old bugger over sixty should be shot," said Ryan. "They are only a menace to society, and should be put down."

"I won't agree with that," said Tinen. "I'll tell you about one of them, seeing as we are on about the subject. Joe Brown the subbie, was telling me a few weeks ago, about an old boy he has with him. One morning there was a lorry of muck to be hand loaded—a damnable job—so he told this young chap to get himself a shovel, and get cracking, saying he would send the old boy to help him. The young buck raised up hell, saying it was not fair as he would have to practically load the wagon himself. Brown just told him to get moving as he had to put old Ned with him because there were no one else available.

"When breakfast time came, and Brown went to the local cafe, the young buck happened to be there as well. 'How is the loading going?' Brown asked him. 'Finished,' he replied. 'Fluking hell, mate, that old geezer can't half work. He's got me knackered. Hell's bells! He wouldn't stop for a breather, just kept on and on like a bleeding robot. Not even a smoke.' 'Now you know,' laughed Brown, 'the tortoise and the hare.'"

"You can't beat having an old boy among the young ones," I said. "Keeps them in check, and it also keeps them working, nice and steady like. Anybody with a shout should always make room for a few, for after all, we will soon be on that train ourselves. I remember a fine strapping young man coming to me once, and asking for the start, but before I could say yes or no, he nodded towards an old boy standing apart, and added, 'Only if he can start too.' It was his father. You tell me who would not start a man like that! Needless to say he was as good as two men on site.

"Yet you have to laugh at them old boys too. They can be very funny, and sure that's an asset to any site. What I'm thinking about was a time in Portsmouth, where I was pit boss on a wartime tunnel job. One Friday morning the general and I were sitting in our hut gazing out the open door, upon the busy yard. Things were going good-style, and we were relaxing with our mugs of tea, when through the yard wandered this lanky old character, coming towards us. On reaching us he leaned up against the door jam, craned his neck round the corner, and asked, 'Anything doing?' He was too old to be a miner, and was unknown to us. I told him he could start right away, if he could bank a crane. An opening at that moment. He could, so I pointed out the crane that was running about the yard and told him to go see the driver.

"Now as he walked away from us, the general pulled out his time book, and shouted after him. 'Hoy mac, what's your name?'

"Damn me, the old clouster stopped dead in his tracts for a moment, then slewed round scratching his head, and answered in a very matter of fact tone: 'Be japers, and I won't know till Monday!' What could you make of that now? Sure everybody knew a lot of people were working on bought books in those days, but cripes who would make it so obvious.

"I never seen anybody laugh so much as that general did, and him a fierce Welshman. There were tears running down his face. Mind you the bucko turned up on Monday with a name that would fill a dictionary, with a few z's thrown in. You would need an encyclopedia to spell it. I'm damn sure you wouldn't give it to a greyhound. That is, if you wanted anybody to back it. Much later I found out that his right name was Finbar."

"They were an innocent lot too," said Mull, "but they were not stupid by any means. Once they seen a thing they had it off, because they took an interest. Young bucks today think they know it all, and don't bother taking any notice of the finer points. Just you ask one of them to do something for you, such as lay a few pipes. He will jump to it right away, then suddenly come to a dead stop: He is lost, and don't know where to start. Yet he may have seen hundreds of pipes laid, but nothing registered, everything was passed off with a shrug of the shoulders. 'Anybody can do that' attitude. Granted most things are simple enough, but they all have that bit of refinement in common. Everything is not as simple as the Hash Sweeney made out, when arguing with this bricklayer in a pub. 'What's in bloody bricklaying—sure when you pick up a brick, you must lay it down.' Some old boys took things far too serious though and were very gullible, thinking everyone was sincere, and accepting most things as gospel. I'll tell you of one such.

"We were working for Balfour Beatty on a wee job, just outside Perth, in Scotland. One of those wartime little things that were done by local gangs. We were picked up every morning at a certain venue, and dropped there again at night. The transport was just an ordinary flat lorry with a small portable canvas and timber shelter carried on the back. It could be offloaded on site, leaving the lorry free for other work.

"This little shelter, or hood as it was called, was used as a site hut to keep our gear in, and when wet we all squeezed inside. Normally we sat round the brazier outside, to have our meals.

"There were eight of us including the ganger. The driver didn't count as he was here and there as required. At the time I'm talking about, we were digging a shallow trench along a hedge that bordered a field of hay. It extended from the road to a little knoll at the top of a sloping field. I think it was for a cable to feed a beacon of some sort on the knoll, as there was an RAF airfield near us, it had something to do with that.

"The day I am talking about was a cold blistery one, gusts of strong wind coming across the fields, forcing the long grass to bow before it. We were fairly comfortable, as we were in the lee of the hedge. The ground being arable, the dig was easy. Nor were there any pressure on us as it was a Ministry job, there was no rush. The old gangerman spent most of his time in the driver's cab, chatting with the driver, or reading. We were having a good crack among ourselves. The usual topics, horses, football, and so forth. Among us there was an old fellow called Phil. A nice old boy who should in fact be retired, were life normal. He had spent all his working years around Perth, never venturing any further. A big innocent man. He was in front of me in the trench, but now, having laid his shovel on the bank, he was making his way up the field along the hedge. We all knew where he was going.

"Among every gang there is always a mischief maker, and we had one by the name of Jim Boyle. A young rascal that kept everyone on their toes, for he was always up to something. Now having watched Phil's departure with more than common interest, he started giving a commentary on his movements, just like one of those radio men. 'He has now located his target. Circling towards it with caution … No flak as yet … Carrying out reconnaissance procedure … stability of ground … wind direction, and force … exposure … absence of ants … bees, wasps … stop … He has now completed a full circle … braces released.' Then he suddenly stopped talking. We all looked round to see what happened or what Boyle was now up to, but he was gone. 'Where is he away to?' I asked Hash Sweeney, who was behind me. 'He is away up the back of the hedge, with his shovel,' replied Sweeney with a shrug, 'whatever he has in mind.' 'Wait and see,' said someone, 'just keep an eye on Phil.'

"We did, but nothing happened. Then Boyle came through the hedge again, jumped into the trench, and carried on digging as before. We were still watching Phil. After a bit Boyle told us what he done. He had slipped up behind the hedge to a point just behind Phil, poked the shovel gently through the hedge in below Phil, and collected. Poor Phil heard nothing, with the wind whistling through the ragged hedge, and with holding on to a tuft of grass to keep his balance, he was fully occupied.

"Now we watched Phil's performance with renewed interest, as he stood up to get back into his harness. It was a long job. After pulling up the trousers, and stuffing them, he had to pick up the loops of the long johns on the brace buttons, then the belt had to come from around the neck, to be buckled on. When he had finished, he stood for a while looking towards the distant hills, as he wiped his nose with the back of his hand. Finally he straightened the peak of his cap with both hands, and stepped out of the ring of trampled grass. After just one step, we seen him stop, turn round, and stare unbelieving at the ground. He had raised his cap, and was scratching his head, as he combed the flattened grass with the toe of his boot. He looked mighty perplexed from where we were. We were in stitches. But damn it all, it was the last straw, when he began to loosen the belt again, lowering the trousers to half mast, and start rummaging inside them. It was the limit, none of us could stand, most were sitting on the bank, bent double. Boyle was at the driver's cab telling them what it was all about, as they watched Phil. Tears were running down the gangers' cheeks.

"After a fruitless search, Phil gave up the ghost altogether, done up the trousers again, and with a last forlorn look, and a kick at the grass, he made his way back to us.

"We were all digging like blazes when he arrived, everyone afraid to look at him. Out of the corner of my eye I could see he was a worried man, a bit white around the gills, you might say. He stepped down in the trench and resumed digging, never saying a word. Nobody else did either, for none could trust themself to do so. After a while young Jim spoke quite casually.

"'Did you enjoy your crap, Phil? A bit stormy for it out in the open, nothing but a hedge for cover. There should be some kind of a portable chemical toilet with a canvas screen round it on site. I saw the soldiers using one, when on manoeuvres.' 'What are you going to do with it when we are finished, and on the move,' asked Sweeney, 'take it with us on the back of the lorry? No thanks! Especially after you lot.' 'Ach!' said a bloke called McCauley, 'sure a bit of weather will harm nobody, especially when enjoying a good relief.'

"That was the cue Boyle was waiting for. 'You know, it is the most natural thing in the world to do, every living thing has to do it, even the king. That's when one is able to do it, but think of the poor buggers that can't do it. I was reading in a book, about people that gets something in the bowels, a kind of lockjaw the other way round, so to speak. It must be terrible. It's said, they start off thinking they had been, when they haven't. They just thought they did. That's how it starts. It's a sort of illusions.'

"Phil was all ears.

"'Must be a terrible disease to have a name like that,' said Sweeney gravely. 'I've heard big words like wheelbarrow, and corrugated iron, but not that one. What do you say Phil?'

"Phil was not interested in Sweeney, as he was looking towards Jim. He asked, 'Where did you read that Jim? You don't get things like that in papers.'

"'Oh, you know the other day when we were rained off? Well I went into the library, to while away the time until the pub opened, and there was this big book on a table. It was a medical book, must have been left out by some student that was reading it. Anyway I started reading it to pass the time so that's one of the things I read.'

"'Damn me that's terrible,' somebody said.

"'Oh worse still,' continued Jim, 'as the disease gets further on, them that has it can't tell when they are needing to go atall. So not knowing, they go about doing it in their trousers, unaware they have done so. Other times they think they have done it when they haven't. Going about messing in your trousers is no fun. Some get wise and have a sack inside their trousers leg, with the top open like a coalbag.'

"'Moy heavens that's terrible,' said Phil, now visibly shaken. 'You go to the bog and think you have when you haven't!'

"'That's about it Phil,' said Jim. Nobody spoke. Everyone was afraid to do so. The ganger was listening as he stood by the trench with his back to it. His shoulders were strangely humped.

"After a while Phil got up out of the trench, put his hand in his pocket, and pulled out some change, then started counting it. As he put it back he remarked very casual like, 'Be dad! I must have dropped some money up there. I better go and have a look for it,' and off he went up the field.

"Well now I need not tell you what we went through, as we watched Phil on his hands and knees rooting among the grass, searching. Three men were on their knees on the bottom of the trench. One man was lying on the bank, while the ganger was in convulsions on the wing of the lorry. I could see nothing through the tears, even though I was looking up the field. Poor Phil was very quiet all day after that, even on the way home, when he was usually quite chirpy. I don't think he ever found out what happened that day so long ago.

"Young Boyle was called up in the army later on, and was killed in Italy."

We enjoyed that story, and as Tom Tinen went for the beer, we visualised the setup that day, and our thoughts were with Boyle for a fleeting moment.

Mull went to the door and looked out, then came back shaking his head. "It's knocking sparks out of the pavement, God knows when will it stop, we'll need web feet if this continues."

"Cripes I thought Ireland and Scotland was bad for rain, but this takes the cake," said Ginger.

"Huh. You never been to South Wales," said Tinen, now back with the drinks. "There's where you see rain. We were once rained off for seven weeks. No not snow or frost, just blinking rain, and no drizzle at that."

"I worked around there myself, and I must agree with Tom. It's wet, but lovely in the summer," I said.

"Wait till I tell you what happened to me down there," said Mull. "I was one time in charge with a contractor who did overhead power lines for the Electricity Board. My job was the foundations, or stub holes as they were called. The holes were quite deep for the bases of those pylons that carried the grid lines. A line of towers is generally kept to rough ground where possible, but passing through arable land cannot always be avoided. Now the damn thing about this was the constant battle with the farmers. You see the Electricity Board right-o-way men, the cunning buggers, did all the yapping, and got the farmer to sign his consent in the middle of winter, when fields were bare. The poor farmer signed, thinking the job was to be done right away, but there goes the snag. When we came along to carry out the work, it was generally in the middle of summer.

"Now you can imagine the kind of a mess we would make of a fine field of corn, or even a nice meadow. With our machinery, concrete mixers, ballast, and timbers. Not to mention a dozen other things, plus truck movements. Oh, you may say, the farmer got well paid for the damages. That's not the point. He may be paid, but he is also human, and a man of the soil into the bargain. How would you like to see your care and attention being pounded into ruin before your eyes. A farmer may seem callous, as regards animals he is everything but. Because beast and land is his bread and butter and also his love in life. Otherwise he would not be a farmer. So one had to see his point when arguing. But the job had to be done. If the cowardly buggers behind it all put a bit of planning into it, all the fuss could have been avoided.

"Well now, we arrived at this farm one Monday morning and found the entrance to the field barred. The big gate was soundly padlocked, and the farmer leaning on it, smoking a pipe, with a pair of corgis yapping at his heels. No amount of persuasion would make him change his mind. Locked the gate would stay. The only course open to me now, was to run into Carmarthen and see my boss. So I jumped into the wagon and off I went.

"They soon sorted it out. They gave me a copy of a letter from the landowners—the farmer was just a tenant—giving me permission to enter the field. I gave this to the farmer on my return, and warned him that he might be sued for expenses caused by the delay. He didn't seem too worried about it, as he unlocked the gate for us. Farmers can be dodgy you know, especially Welsh ones. I was once chased out of a field with a pitchfork at my arse.

"We now entered the field, and began the usual performance of setting up. The farmer forgotten for the time being anyway. We were busy, but unknown to us so was the farmer. Suddenly I heard a shout. Hoy, look! It was one of the boys shouting as he legged it for the back of the truck. We all looked around for the cause of all the panic. Cripes! There was a huge brown bull coming tearing down the field, making straight for us and roaring its head off. Needless to say we nearly beat the young fellow to the truck. He stopped about twenty yards from us, and went down on his knees, to start tearing hell out of the ground with his horns. He was sending divots flying left, right, and centre. After I got my breath back, I tapped on the roof of the driver's cab, and told him to head for the gate, where the old coot of a farmer was leaning on it, smoking his pipe, and watching all the fun. I kicked up hell with him, and pointed out our right to be there. I ordered him to remove the bull.

"He just took his pipe from his mouth, and looked at me quite calmly. 'Oh, I agree man,' he said. 'By that bit o' paper you showed me. Indeed to goodness man you have every right to. So to get a bit of peace and quiet, go show him the letter, then he will have to leave you alone.'

"Do you know, I had to get a policeman out from Narbeth to get him to move that bull. He explained to the policeman that it was not his fault the bull couldn't read.

"I may have won the fight, but the laugh was on me. Every farm I went on after that, I was asked if I had a letter for the bull. In a way it was all to the good, it gave the community a good laugh, and broke the ice for me. I never had one bit of bother after that. So now you know what can happen down there. Lovely people indeed."

"Sure the people there are just like ourself, there isn't much difference between the Irish, Scots, and Welsh. All much the same," said Tinen. "They like a bit of micky taking, and make every story twice as long in the telling, which takes to mind, Pat. Do you remember Duggie MacClure that was in Killin with us?"

"Oh. Cripes why would I not, the bugger. He was a droll character, was Duggie. An Oban man."

"Of course, he only went navvying when there was no fishing. He really enjoyed his spells at it, and could tell a good yarn too. Was he not at sea during the war?"

"Indeed and that he was, and went through the mill too. He was in the merchant navy, and did four trips to Russia on the convoys. Afterwards he got married and took a job on one of the island ferries as he wanted to be near home, but as the family came along the pay was too low, so he went back to the fishing and the navvying during the closed season. He could tell the tale."

"That's what I was coming to," said Tinen. "When I said that him, and his kind were like ourselves. He was telling about an old skipper who was with the ferry company for donkey's years. Up and down the coast among the islands. Apparently whenever he got in jeopardy with his ship, he always consulted a matchbox he carried in his waistcoat pocket. Everybody from the cabin boy to the mate wondered over the years about what he had in the box. Some said it was a Saint Christopher medal, others maintained it was a lucky mascot. Nobody knew.

"Well one day, didn't he take some kind of a seizure, while in Oban, and was taken away to the hospital. Now the mate took command of the ship temporary like. At last there came a chance to solve the greatest mystery of all times. What was in the box. When the mate went to pack the skipper's clothing and things, the whole crew of four gathered in his cabin to witness the phenomenon. The matchbox was found, and reverently opened. What was in it! Nothing, but written on the bottom was: 'Red is Port. Green is Starboard!' The old bugger."

"Moy jases," said Mull. "That was a nice character to be in charge of a boat, didn't know his right from his left."

"Ach!" said Ryan. "There are plenty people like that. I once heard of a mam that turned up for work wearing a pair of wellies with 'Mowlem' on one boot and 'Wimpey' on the other, and when remarked upon by some wag, was told that there was nothing quaint about them, as he had a similar pair at home."

"Talking about footwear," smiled Tinen, "reminds me of a fellow on a certain job who was always complaining about his boots hurting him, until one day somebody asked him what size he took. Size nine, he answered. But those you are wearing look more like eights, remarked the questioner. I know, he answered, but I have a mountain of debts. I am being evicted from the house for rent arrears. There is a court order against me for assaulting her. The tally men are watching every move I make, in case I bail out. So the only pleasure I have in life, is getting home, and taking these bloody boots off."

"Do you know, Tom Tinen," said Ryan, "it is no use blaming you for being a stranger to the truth, not when you have been so long in Pat's company. You are now beyond help. Yet there was an old boy in my place who lost a leg in the Battle of Mons. I think he was with the Munsters.* However, he had a good pension from the British Army, which he collected every Thursday—that was his day on the binge.

"There was a pub-cum-shop in the village, which was a common practice in Ireland, and still is in certain places. One side the bar, the other side a shop, with haberdashery in between. You could buy anything from a needle to an anchor there.

"The old owner usually sat on a chair by the door, during the summer months, chatting to everybody as they came in, and to anybody passing by, that had the time to.

"This Thursday while on his usual perch, he heard from over his shoulder the old soldier telling the barman-cum-shopkeeper that he wanted to buy a new boot.

"'A boot!' said he, as he swung round on his chair. 'A boot! Do you think I am going to spoil a good pair of boots, to give you one!' He was well aware that the longer they kept debating the longer he was keeping the soldier drinking, and from going elsewhere with his money.

"'What would I be doing with a pair,' said the soldier. 'Me with just one foot, and a lump of wood for another.' So they argued for a long while before the old soldier had to surrender.

---

* Royal Munster Fusiliers

"'Right,' mumbled the old barman-cum-shopkeeper, nodding towards a pile of shoe boxes that were stacked against the shop counter. 'Get yourself over there and pick a pair.'

"The old soldier did this. While he examined the boots he kept grumbling about lack of consideration. Eventually he made his final selection, paid for them, and staggered on his way, singing one minute, then cursing about having to duke shells for old bastards of bootsellers the next minute.

"It was to be a month before the bootseller found out he had taken two left boots from among the boxes. Thus spoiling two pair of boots on him."

"Serve the old shopkeeper right," said Mull, "though one could not expect him to split a pair. Anyway the old soldier, true to form, pulled a fast one, and good luck to him."

"I think I'll do a bit of shopping while there's a lull at the counter," said Ryan as he made for the bar.

"No whiskey for me," I shouted, "and Ryan will give you a hand."

"That beer is dead flat," grumbled Mull, as he screwed up his old face. "He is dishing out slops."

"By the prices he charges there is no need for slops, for he is making a fortune as it is, but like a lot more landlords he is not satisfied with that," I said.

"Talking about landlords," added Ryan, as he sat down after paying for the drinks. "I'll tell you about one who used to have the Grey Bear outside Chester. I forget the name of the village, but no matter. The pub was about a mile out. We were in the locality digging transmission-line stanchion holes, for a subbie. As you know, those holes stretch over a long distance, so working in pairs we were well scattered along the line. The wagon collected my mate and I every night outside the Bear, as we were working nearby. My mate was a bloke named Jackie Leeming, who hailed from Barrow-in-Furness. Sometimes we had to wait quite a while as the wagon had to negotiate some terrible places to pick up the men. So we usually went in for a pint while waiting.

"This evening we entered just as he was opening the doors. Being a cold November evening, as I ordered and waited for service, Jackie went to the fire, and picked up the poker to give it a stir. Now right enough you don't do that to a newly topped-up coke fire. You have to leave it to congeal.

Jackie was a bit thick in his ways. 'Leave the bloody fire alone,' shouted the landlord. 'If it needs poking, I'll do it.' He appeared to be a bit on edge.

"When I got to the table where Jackie was seated, he was also in a bad mood. 'Fuck him, and his fire,' he said. I explained to him how he would only bugger up the fire by poking it, but he would not have it. However the wagon came after a while, and that was that.

"We didn't get in there again for a few days as we were working elsewhere, but we did on the following Friday evening and it was the landlady who served us. 'Where is the cock tonight?' asked Jackie. 'Oh,' she said, 'he has gone into town to see that new film just out. *Twenty Thousand Leagues Under the Sea*. Being an ex-submariner he has been dying to see it.'

"Now I started chatting to her as she was a very nice woman, and very interested in what we were doing. She was also very good-looking. I was paying no attention to Jackie until I heard the door bang. I looked round to see who came in, thinking it might be the rest of the gang, seeing it was a Friday night, but there were nobody there but Jackie. However, we chatted for a while longer as the wagon was late. I was just on the verge of joining Jackie at the table when the door flew open, and there stood the landlord. 'What's the matter?' he asked the startled wife. 'No … othing!' she managed to stutter. 'I thought you were at the pictures.' 'I was,' he said. 'But a flash came on the screen telling me to come home immediately.'

"'Oh, I did that,' said Jackey, calm as you like. 'The fire needs poking.' Which it did I noticed. Well I'll tell you something else, I didn't get a chance to notice much more for we were lucky to get out of there alive. Were it not for the fact that the wagon driver tooted for us at that moment, and the landlord was well aware of a wagonful of men who would pull the place apart on the slightest provocation, he would have maimed us."

"Leeming must have phoned the cinema manager while you were chatting up the landlady," said Mull. "It was a damnable trick to pull."

"That Leeming bloke would remind you of the tramp Malone, if you remember him," said Tinen.

"Oh, indeed we do," answered Mull. "By cripes he would do it right enough, and wouldn't run afterwards as he would probably talk his way out of it. For he could talk."

"You can say that again," agreed Tinen. "He was the greatest talker I have ever heard. He obviously had a good education."

"Well," I said. "Being reminded of him brings to mind something he told me regarding being on tramp one time, down around Slough, or Reading."

"Could you believe him though?" questioned Ryan. "He was known to say more than his prayers."

"I know that, but it is worth telling, and doing so in his own kind of way. He told me: 'I was on tramp, and making for the big smoke. Having spent the previous night under a hedge just outside Reading, for summer weather it was cool enough, though I gave myself a good shake, however come noon it turned out a glorious day, the sun splitting the rocks, as one might say. I was dandering along nice and steady like when I began to feel a bit hungry so I decided to drum up in the woods bordering the road. I gathered some kindling and made a fire to boil my drum, then with the drum of tea and a cob of bread and cheese I sat back against a tree to enjoy it. Suddenly through the wood came this man carrying a gun, with a pair of lovely dogs at his heels. A gamekeeper I thought right away, and he will have me for something, even if it is only trespassing. "Who are you, and what are you doing here?" he asked, in a very cultured voice. I knew then right away that he was no gamekeeper. "Oh," said I. "I'm just a tramp navvy passing through to a job in London. Sure the smell of the lonesome pine beckoned me, and it made me so hungry I decided to brew up." "Brew up!" said he. "I have not heard that term since my army days. Could I by any chance have a drink of your tea please?" "Sure, help your-self sir," I said, handing him the drum, after wiping the edge with a bit of cheesecloth. Then I made a fuss of the dogs. It's policy to make any friends you can when in a fix. Dammit man he finished my tea, as he questioned me about the navvying life. He gave me the impression of a man yearning for something he missed in life. When he finished he thanked me, adding, "That was the nicest tea I ever drank, can you give me your name please?" I did. "Wait there," he said, "I'll be back in a moment," and off he went. Now I was swithering whether to make a run for it or not, thinking he might have gone for the police, but I decided against it as he seemed too much of a gent to do a shabby trick like that. Sure enough he came back after a while, and handed me a rolled-up piece of paper. Then wishing me luck he disappeared the way he came. By japers I wasn't long after him for I wanted to get well away from there, just in case. About two miles up the road I decided to sit down on the side of a ditch, and have a squint at what he gave me as I knew it wasn't money. Lords a daisy! when I opened it. What do you think it was, but a parchment. True as heaven, a roll of parchment with the following statement written in beautiful lettering: "This gives the bearer Patrick Aloysius John Malone the rights to 'Brew Up' anywhere in the British Isles." Signed and sealed, the Prince of Wales. Now then! What do you make of that, Pat?'

"I was dumfounded. 'Wait! You haven't heard the end of it,' he continued, raising his hand before I could say anything. 'I was passing through Piccadilly, sometime afterwards, when I decided to put theory to the test. So I planted myself down in front of yon statue, gathered some bits and pieces that were lying around, and started to make a fire, to brew up. Oh, it wasn't long before a copper came along, and ordered me in no mean terms, to sling my hook. I handed him my parchment, which he read with a frown. That put a flea in his ear. He no sooner had it read than he was on the blower to headquarters. Sure enough after a while a police car came screeching up, and out jumped this fellow with the peak of his cap smothered in scrambled eggs. He read the parchment while glancing at me sitting there like a maharaja. Then he calmly rolled it up, and handed it to me as he turned to the sergeant driver, and said, "Nip over to Hyde Park, Charles, quick as you can, and gather up some sticks to help this man get his drum boiled, so we can get him out of here." He did it too.'

"That's Malone's tale, and he stuck to it."

"Well by cripes! Didn't I say he said more than his prayers," said Ryan, shaking his head. "That bastard would lie his way into heaven."

"I don't know," added Mull gravely. "He could have been telling the truth—stranger things have happened you know. I know for a fact one thing he told me was true."

"Ach, sure you would believe anything," said Ryan with a shrug. "We all know that. Why wouldn't he tell you a yarn, it's not every day he comes across a galoot with his mouth open."

"If a man tells you something, you don't necessarily have to believe it," I said, "but you listen, and providing it is feasible, that is sufficient—you may doubt it, but certainly can't disprove it. For instance the Yank Brown was telling us once about the things he saw when up in the Yukon. He reckoned it was so cold one time he saw a dog stuck to a tree, probably but most improbable."

"Holy jases! I'm getting out of here," said Ryan, rising. "Between Malone having the half of Scotland Yard gathering kindlings for him, to brew up in the heart of London, never mind having such an insignificant character like the Prince of Wales slugging tay from his half-burnt-out drum, along comes another herbert that sees a dog who's having a quiet piss getting himself welded to a tree! Jases it's time to go."

"Sit down and listen ye damn clouster ye," said Tinen. "You might find yourself a bit educated at the end of the day, and not be running about like a jackass all your life. After all you might have to sing for your supper one day, and what use the singer without a song."

"Ignore that stupid bugger," said Mull, nodding towards Ryan. "The man told me this in his own words: 'I happened to be in a pub in Liverpool in 1940, and in great form, telling the tale to a gang of seamen that were about to sail. Being sailors they enjoyed a good yarn, and furthermore, not being sure of a return ticket, they were spending. Later on after they departed, and I was alone, this fellow appeared at my side as if from nowhere. Wearing a blue uniform, with gold on the peak of his cap. He addressed me: "I was listning to you there, and I can see you are unfit for the services"—the bloody cheek of him—"so I could offer you a good job, as you can talk." "What doing?" I asked warily. "Announcing trains up at Lime Street Station," he replied. "You see we are stuck, as all the regulars have been called up." "I'm your man. When do I start?" I asked. "Tomorrow," he said. "If you give me your name." "Patrick. Aloysius. John. Malone," says I—'"

"Not interrupting," said Ryan. "But in the name of jases, where did he get those names from! It must have taken a bloody week to baptise him. Carry on."

Mull ignored him. "'Well,' said Malone, 'after reporting on the following morning, I was taken into this office, and given a brand-new navy suit. The first suit I've worn in twenty years. Then I was taken upstairs to a wee box room with a big window, so you could see all the trains. There was a table with some papers scattered on it. A microphone, and a comfortable-looking chair. A big blackboard was nailed to the wall, with a list of train departure times, and destinations scribbled on it. The bloke who took me there was like a cat on a hot plate, didn't seem to want any responsibility for me, and couldn't get away fast enough, saying they were fierce busy with war trains, and not enough staff to cope. Before you could say Jack Robinson I was on my own, to make the best of it. Of course I should have been given some training, but they had a brand-new war on their hands.

"'I had a good look around, as I took a swig from my pocket bottle, just to clear the brain. I looked up the first train due out, and seen it was the nine forty-five for London. Plenty time to have another good slug. One needs that when one is in such an important job. By japers if my old mother could only see me now in this flash suit, with a glossy peaked cap to match, and me making important announcements, just like a radio man. Wouldn't she be the proud woman. Not to mention them other clowns, up and down the country digging large holes. That was over for me now. Time for another swig.

"'At last seeing the train was due out in ten minutes' time, I decided it was time I put a bit of a gimp on myself, and throw myself about as a man would say. In other words, to get cracking. Fuck the papers, sure I know this country inside out, what would I be needing papers for. Anybody would think that I had never been to London before. So I started: "The train now standing at platform two is the nine forty-five for London. Euston. Calling at all stations down the line: Birkenhead. Chester. Stoke-on-Trent, and Darby … Leicester. Northampton. Bedford. Letchworth and Welwyn. Then, Watford. Barnet, and Euston in London. All aboard that's going aboard." That's the way to do it. Dammit I deserve another drop of the fortification before repeating that.

"'Now I just made one little mistake. Do you see, I was never on an express train in my life, so the way the trains went and the way I went were two different ways. Trains don't have to look for work! Also I overlooked the fact that the train was a nonstop to London, and moreover, that there were three hundred dockers from Birkenhead over in Liverpool, at a morning union meeting, with threepenny return tickets. The fluking lot piled on the train and landed down in Euston. As the only trains back to Liverpool that day were troop and ammunition trains, it cost the London Midland Railway a fortune to bed them down for the night, and cart them back next morning. When I was called out of my box by Scrambled Eggs's beckoning forefinger, I must admit he looked a lot healthier than he did the previous day. His face looked stouter, and it had more colour to it. He didn't have a lot to say either. Just a couple of words: "Get that fucking suit off, Malone, right now." I was rained off there and then.'

"I should think so too," added Mull.

"Did any of you ever see him do a bit of work?" asked Tinen. "I haven't. Always around jobs, yes, but never on them."

"Oh. He worked with me a few times," I said. "A good worker too. Never had much to say when doing so, and that was a blessing. After dinner when he had his few pints, and the job's back been broken, with everything easing off a bit, he would have something to say right enough. One afternoon as we were poodling about, he reckoned to us that he was the only man ever to scaffold a pig."

"Be cripes," said Mull. "I've seen Saint Paul's, Nelson's Column, and Big Ben scaffolded, but I have yet to see a pig scaffolded."

"Apparently he was doing a job for a certain Lady Ardle on her estate, somewhere on the Scottish border. How he came to be there I will never know. Just as nobody will ever know how he got anywhere, but he did. Her being the wife of some big construction company's chairman might come into the reckoning somewhere. However, as we all know Malone, he got well in with the lady, and she thought the world of him, and was forever seeking his opinions. So not surprising she came to him one day worried about a sow she had on the place. The last time she littered, she killed the lot by lying on top of them. Some sows do that if they are young animals. The lady was now asking Malone what she should do to prevent a recurrence, as the sow was due again. Malone told her to leave it in his capable hands, that she had nought to worry about, which pleased her no end.

"Malone, like the hangman that he was, weighed up his prisoner. After he had a good squint at her he reckoned she had an evil eye in her head beneath a flappy ear, and would do in the piglets again given half a chance. So he decided to keep a weather eye on her when she started to perform.

"To be prepared, he gathered up a rake of putlogs and scaffold clamps that were lying about the place. So when the sow started to litter on the following day Malone was ready, and went to town on her there and then, caging her in an upright position with a frame of putlogs. He made it so she could relax and rest on the cross ties, but leave enough room for the little pigs to get between her and the ground to feed. He must have made a good job of it too. For the sow appeared quite content. The little pigs were quite content, and the Lady Ardle was quite content. So everybody lived happy ever after. That's how he came to scaffold a pig."

"Trust him," said Mull. "Nowadays you can get a frame for that, but not in Malone's time I suppose—perhaps he was the one who invented it. Who knows."

"The only thing that bugger ever invented was lies," said Tinen. "One of his funny yarns to me was about an old uncle he reckoned he had. Somewhere back in Offaly where he came from long ago. This old uncle was a bachelor, and lived on his own. It seems a certain Yank had bought a cottage near him and was busy doing it up. Malone's shack, being an old thatched place, was falling apart, and he would never do anything about it. Local authority offered him another place, but he would not leave the old homestead, in spite of the roof being nearly gone.

"One day the Yank came into the pub where old Malone drank regularly, and ordered a scotch. The landlord, as always anxious to butter up to a Yank, asked how the renovation was getting on. 'Mighty fine,' said the Yank. 'All I need now is the water and light in, and everything will be tickittyboo.'

"Old Malone turned to his drinking mate. 'Listen to that bastard, and his tickittybooing. Him wanting the light and water in, and me up all winter trying to keep the fluking two of them out.'"

"I wonder where he is now," said Mull. "I mean the younger one. I haven't heard of him for years. No doubt he is around somewhere."

"A lot of them ends up with the nuns, I believe," said Tinen. "The May Morning and Long John Freel did. I met a few down around Torquay, they like the south coast for its climate, and furthermore the local cider is cheap in comparison to any other place. Personally I like the south too."

"I worked down south." I added, "In Portsmouth, as I have told you already. A good town for the working man. We were tunneling in Portsdown Hill. Oil tanks, and ammunition dumps for the Royal Navy. That hill is like a rabbit warren. The pubs were lively as indeed all navalport pubs are, always full of women. A lot of the boys shackled up there, and stayed on after we left. Some ended up in the navy."

"The ground would be good around that area," suggested Ryan.

"Oh, it was. Chalk, you could tunnel forever without using a stick, but that would be your downfall. Chalk is not like rock where you can spot weak fissure and scale it off or bring it down. Chalk on the other hand may look as sound as a bell, then suddenly away it comes, giving no warning atall, especially after the air gets at it. Did you ever come across Mad Forker on your travels, Mull?"

"Indeed I did, up in Norwich long ago. He was some flower."

"Well he was there when I was there. In fact he was in my gang, along with the Sinker and the Slurry. We were all in digs around Stamshaw. There was a camp over by Fareham, but nobody liked it. Digs were better, and just as cheap. The crack was good on Saturday nights among the ladies."

"Some fast ladies about the same town too," said Mull. "Most of the professional ones were nicknamed after battleships, the biggest after aircraft carriers, but you mentioned the Mad Forker, Pat. I suppose he was a miner then, for he was a good one in his day. A rough old bugger in many ways, but a sound bloke when off the cider. I once heard a story about him and the miner McCale, when they knocked about London. The pair of them spent most of their time around yon cider house on the Edgware Road, and it was there the miner met this old broiler, and married her. She didn't have any money that anybody knew of. Nor was she anything to look at, but then neither was the miner. Him and Forker went their separate ways after that. A month or two after the wedding, for some unknown reason, she went and borrowed a silk scarf from one of the neighbours, and hung herself behind the door. A damnable trick to do.

"Some time later Forker and a buddy, the miner O'Dowd, were going along the Edgware Road one Sunday morning, when who did he see on the other side of the street, but the brave McCale. Forker told O'Dowd about what happened, suggesting they go across and extend their condolences. This they did. The Forker shook hands with McCale. 'Sorry about your troubles. I heard the wife made a plumb bob of herself behind the door.' A nice way to put it! It was the mate that told me."

"That's like him right enough," said Tinen, a real old miner. He was with us once on some job somewhere, I can't remember where, but we came in one morning to find all the tools outside the toolbox, and Forker sleeping inside. 'Why should they have a roof over their heads, and me sleeping out,' he maintained. The foreman didn't agree with him though, and ran him."

"I don't know how that O'Dowd could talk about Forker, for he was worse than him, and they were mates for years," I said. "They were both in Aberdare when I was there. He was the thickest clouster of a man I ever came across, and that's saying something. He was married himself I believe, somewhere back in Ireland, but they never got on, hence the reason he spent most of his time here. I was told about one of his rare visits there. No doubt to do the damage, as usual. On his arrival some locals called in to see him, as he would have a bottle with him. At that time he was working on some tunnel job somewhere up north, and as his visitors had messed around in tunnels too in their time, that's what the crack was all about.

"When they had all gone home, the old wife asked him, 'John, what kind of an animal is the shield?' Now I am only repeating what I have been told. 'Jases! Woman, don't you know anything atall?' he shouted, as he leapt off the chair. 'Come here.' He beckoned her along to the old-fashioned dresser that stood opposite the door. 'Right now, that's the shield.' He pointed to the dresser. 'Now you are my labourer, so get behind me for I'm going to put a bit of left lead on the shield.' 'OK,' she nodded nervously. The old bugger then got a hold of the dresser to yank one side away from the wall, but with the old concrete floor being a bit rough, as he dragged the dresser it rocked with vibration, shaking loose one of the ornamental plates that is common to the top shelf of all dressers. The poor woman, seeing the top plate of the family heirloom about to come the Humpty Dumpty on the floor, dived forward to catch it, but was grabbed by the shoulder, and slung across the floor. 'Get back there!' he roared. 'It's flukers like you that gets hurt in big workshops like this.' Now would anybody wonder if she was glad to see the back of him."

"Not in the least," agreed Tinen. "Thick enough for anything. What time is it, Pat?"

"Oh, we have another half hour to go."

"You would think some of them old buggers that spent so much time about this world would have got wise in their old age," said Ginger. "The tykes who return to where they came from, to retire, were six times worse than those who never left. Being away so long, local people thought they were knowledgeable, which they should be. They were regarded as an authority on all subjects, and rather than admit ignorance of somethings, they went and made a balls up of it.

"I was told of a clouster called Coll Gallagher who retired back home after a period of misspent years as a gangerman in this country. By what I was told, his wife would have made the general foreman's grade had she been around. The following mishap occurred when she was away in Glasgow, visiting a married daughter who lived there. All Donegal people have somebody to visit in Glasgow. And those in Glasgow, like the Muslims going to Mecca, do a pilgrimage to Donegal at least once. When Coll got her away for a spell, he was quite happy and content messing about the place. One fine day he was trimming grass along this dry ditch with a billhook, his mind miles away as scutching grass needs little concentration. Suddenly he was jerked back to reality, by an almighty fluttering and a squawking coming from the ditch. On searching for the root of it, didn't he find the wife's pet hen, a little red one, kicking up hell on the bottom of the ditch. She had her reasons, for hadn't he scutched the leg of her.

"In the summertime, hens have a habit of going back to nature, and laying out. That's what she was up to. Now to add insult to injuries she was also the best layer about the place. So you see the predicament he was in as he made for the house with the hen under his oxter, and the severed leg in his hand. What was he going to do! She would have his guts for garters on her return in a fortnight's time.

"Didn't I tell you he had been away for many years! So there had to be a way out of it. A man of his standing had to have an answer. Eureka! He got it. A transplant. Well, a replant would be more to the point. He placed the hen on the kitchen table, and looked around for the requirements. Splints? Two spoons would do nicely. Bandages? Ach, a piece of rag would do. Then he found a piece of sticking plaster, and a tin of boracic ointment. *Japers*, he thought to himself, *you could do a major operation with less.* After he fixed the leg back on the stump, he lowered the hen onto the floor. She looked sound enough, just a bit of a wobble, maybe too much bandaging. Dammit she would have to do.

"Well, a fortnight soon passed and the day of reckoning had arrived. The charger being due back the following day, it was now or never for the red hen. If the leg was not OK, then the fox would have to take the blame. Damn me man! When he stripped the bandages off, the hen was as right as rain. Just a funny walk.

"The man who told me also maintained that she soon started laying again, even though Coll made a minor bloomer. You see, in the excitement, didn't he fix the leg on the wrong way round.

"You would think that would dampen any man's spirit. But no, not Coll's. He went about boasting that she was the finest hen about the place, maintaining that you could never tell if she was in the corn or not, because as she dug with one foot she was backfilling with the other."

"Oh dear Lord above! If by any chance you happen to have Malone up there, send him down please," cried Ryan in agony. "No wonder it's raining. Perhaps another flood might be in order."

"If it's the flood you are expecting then it's all aboard the ark, for old Noah behind the ramp is ringing the last bell," said Mull.

"Well," I said, "the rain seems to be easing off, so we better get on our ways. Perhaps we'll see you in Hammersmith tonight, Mull. I heard you were going visiting there."

He never answered, just cocked a thumb as we parted.

Chapter 5

"Damn the man, we should never have started work this morning atall—now we are soaking wet, for nothing. We only get our guaranteed hours, and have worked most of them," said Ryan, sourly.

"Ach, stop your grumbling," said Mulholland. "The GF was only doing what he is paid for. You haven't been on the site two minutes, and you are grumbling already. The worst day's work you ever done, Pat, was starting that whiner. I don't know what you are grumbling about. You are in the pub—what more do you want."

"A dry arse," replied Ryan.

"You haven't had that since your last nappy," sniggered Mull.

After yesterday's snow followed by a night of rain, the morning came in sullen and cold with heavy clouds on the sideline, biding their time. As McGonagall the pelter remarked, "Just waiting to catch us on the hop, and then drown us." He was right, for it opened up again at noon, when we had most of the site mopped up. So back to square one.

"Cheltenham starts tomorrow," muttered Tom Tinen, as he studied the racing pages. "Some money gets spent there, so it does. Them rich Irish farmers over in droves, and loaded with money, yet at home they never stop pleading poverty. What they spend on the course, I believe, is nothing to what they spend gambling in the hotels. Up till all hours playing poker, yet if you worked for the bastards back home, you wouldn't have an arse in your trousers."

"I have never been on an Irish farm," said Mull. "But nevertheless, farmers are the same all over the world, misery guts. A lot of your Irish farmers own racehorses, and are well in the know. When they come across, they won't tell you, though, in case you might make a few bob. If they were ghosts, they wouldn't give you a fright. Them trainers, especially the Irish lot, are worse still—wee boys with catapults hidden in hedges, to hit a horse where it hurts as he passes. The jockeys are no better, who can tell when they pull a horse. A man who knew the racing fraternity told me about a stable lad who came over here once.

"The trainer he worked for over there had lost his licence, so he had to go. He soon got fixed up with another one over here, as experienced stable lads are hard to find. Now one day when attending a certain race meeting, where the stable had a few running, he was spotted by no other than Lord Fotherington himself, giving something to a horse he was leading out. The same lord being a steward of the course collared him right away. 'What have you given that horse?' he demanded. 'Ach. Sure and it's only a cube of sugar to quieten him down, sir,' says our man, taking two more cubes out of his pocket. 'Look, you have one of them, sir, and I'll have the other. Just plain sugar.' 'Well,' said the lord, taking the sugar, 'but you don't do that over here. So don't let me catch you doing it again.'

"As our bold fellow reached the track, and was giving the jockey his final instructions before letting the horse go, he tells him, 'Now hold him back on a tight rein until you reach the last furlong, then let the fucker go, and you have nothing to worry about atall. If anything passes you, then it will either be me or Lord Fotherington.'"

"I don't doubt that for a fact," said Tom Tinen. "The Irishman takes his horses very serious indeed. I read once about a well-known Lord who wrote in his memoirs about a time he went over to Kildare to buy a certain horse, it was in the troubled days. However, later on in years, after Ireland had its independence he was attending some function in London, where the Irish were also represented. It so happened that while having a drink, one of the Irishmen present reminded him of it, and named the horse he intended to buy, that morning. Said the Irishman, 'You were not aware that when you tried it over some fences, there were two of us hiding behind a hedge waiting for you. To shoot you.' 'Damn it, I never knew,' said the surprised lord. 'And may I ask why you didn't?' 'Ach,' said the

Irishman, 'sure when we saw the bad bargain you were getting, we didn't have the heart to.' That's how serious they take their horses there."

"Dogs and horses are a curse," said Ginger. "Many a man met his Waterloo gambling, but strangely enough, it seems to be the worst off who do most of the gambling. Go to the poorest part of any town, and you will find the bookie is the busiest man there, apart from the debt collector. I once heard there was a bookie in Dundee who took jam jars. Just imagine placing a bet of two jam jars each way on some nag in the two thirty at Redcar. Of course they told me there was a snag in it, the bookie paid you out in jam jars, or as they call them in Scotland, jeely jars."

"Go to hell," said Mulholland. "I have no doubt you have gathered a few jam jars in your time, but as for a bookie taking them, even if worth a penny each, is bunkum. A lot of people don't know they had betting shops in Scotland long before England, granted they were illegal, but they were wide open. The police used to raid them once a year, coming along with a bus, and just loaded everybody up, and took them to the police station. Whatever they were fined, generally ten bob, the bookie paid it. It was always referred to as the bookie's annual outing.

"Do you remember, Pat," asked Mulholland, "yon tea boy we had up in Dornoch? Bill Matheson was his name I think. By crikey, he could spin some yarns in the pub, or even out of it for that matter. He was an old sailor, and a great tea boy."

"Yes he was all that Mull, and came from Wester Ross, I believe. The only person to my knowledge that could stand a chance against him would be the tramp Malone. No matter what you talked about he could go one better. The boys used to play hell on him, though. One morning at breaktime, he had the drums boiled as usual. All in a line on an old railway sleeper, ready for you to add your tea and sugar, his own drum included. When the lads got his back turned, he was in the office with the foreman's tea, they emptied his drum, and nailed it to the sleeper, from inside, then refilled it. When old Bill tried to lift his drum the sleeper wanted to come too, he went mad. Another morning, somebody got hold of his sandwiches, and removed the cheese, then replaced it with raw turnip slices, as there was a field of turnips nearby. Bill took a mouthful, then another one before he spat it out. 'I just think that damn landlady of mine has lost a few slates,' he said, examining his bread. 'I'm damn sure that's turnips she's given me on my piece.' 'Nobody would give a working man turnips on his piece,' somebody said. 'Well you just taste that,' Bill asked him. 'Does she think I'm a bloody cow?'

"I think he fell out with his landlady that night, for he moved in with the widow MacCloud the next day."

"He deserved all he got for telling so many blooming lies," said Mull. It was the crack about racing that reminded me of him. Wait till you hear this yarn he told us one night in the pub. It was a stormy winter's night, with all of us gathered round a roaring fire, one could tolerate anything for the crack, as everybody was contented. Somebody mentioned horse riding, and jockeys, how dangerous it was, when Matheson remarked, in his soft West Highland lilt, 'Did I ever tell you that I was once a jockey?' 'No,' said Willie MacCaskel, grinning, a proper rascal of a lad, who also hailed from the west coast and a bugger for winding Bill up. 'I thought you were just a seaman, Bill.' 'Ach man, it was just before I ever went to sea. I was jockey for Westie.* Oh, I rode a lot of winners for him, sure enough, the best one was in the Derby. A four-year-old mare called The Sparrow Hawk.' 'You must have been famous then,' said MacCaskel. 'Indeed yes, but I never let it go to my head, like some people. I just slipped away to sea after that Derby. I couldn't stand the fuss of it all. But to tell you about the race, we started off right enough, at a terrible fast gallop, but none of the others were a match for The Sparrow Hawk, she was leaving them miles behind. We were going full steam ahead rounding that Tattenham Corner headland, and I taking a look astern to see where they were, when damn me, didn't she stop dead! Why? you might well ask. Because she foaled! There and then, right in the middle of the course, and under the very nose of old Westie himself.

"'Och, sure the whole field went by us like the charge of the light brigade, but man oh man, The Sparrow Hawk was not beaten yet, not by a long chalk. Up with her on her feet, and away with us after the rest of the field, we caught up with them, and passed them like the fires of hell, just as if they were standing. I just got a glimpse of the winning post flashing by like fork lightning. We had won, now don't you think that was a grand thing to do?' After a while MacCaskel managed to speak: 'Aye just so, it

---

* *Westie* was the local nickname for the Duke of Westminster, who owned most of the land in the area.

was a grand thing sure enough, but what happened to the foal, Bill?' 'Ach. He just came in second.'"

"Holy blazes," said Ryan. "I've heard them all now, that takes the cake right enough. Did he expect you to believe that crack?"

"Well he believed it himself," I said, grinning. "Sure what could you say to a man who told us once that during the Battle of Jutland, he spewed up the whole lining of his stomach, two zinc pailfuls, he said. When asked how he got over it, he told us he sucked a lump of tarry rope, to give it a new sort of lining, while he kept on firing the guns, and damn the bit of bother it's given him since."

"I'm fluked if I would follow him to the prowie," said Mull.

"True enough, there are some people who believe themselves," said Tom Tinen. "We had a character like that working with us in this quarry, and he believed whatever he said was the God's truth. He came from somewhere in Fifeshire, and you know what they say, 'It takes a lang spoon tac sup wae a Fifer.' Though I liked working among them, for I found them sincere folk. However this bugger maintained that he once fell down a pit shaft while repairing it, a hundred and eighty fathoms, and landed on top of the cage, which broke his fall. Injuries? No none, he just burst his bootlaces."

"You know something," said Ryan. "I have yet to meet a Highlander that couldn't tell the tale. Perhaps they are gifted in that respect, as some folk maintain. I think they are just so aware of life, that they see a funny side to everything in it, without the whisper of a smile. They couldn't describe a funeral without giving it a twist of humour, maybe unaware of it. Even their everyday life is softly touched by it. Do you remember Duggie MacClure, on that job in Dornoch, Pat?"

"I do indeed. He had been a seaman too, in his youth."

"He told us about the fellow from Ullapool who paid off the same ship as him, in Glasgow. Apparently they went on the binge, which was common practice among seamen. On the following morning when they woke up in the sailor's home, Ullapool was concerned that he had brought nothing home from abroad for his old mother. However, later on in the day when on their way to catch their trains, they happened to pass a pet shop, and Duggie spotted a tortoise lying motionless in the window. He suggested Ullapool should buy it, saying, as his mother had never seen such a thing, he could say he brought it home from darkest Africa for her. The tortoise was bought.

"Duggie now reckoned he didn't meet his shipmate for about two years afterwards, and it was then he inquired as to how his mother took to the tortoise. 'Ach,' he said. 'Sure I told her he was used to heat, and to keep him near the fire, which she did. It was on my next visit home that I asked about it. "That!" she said. "Ach, sure it never stops sleeping, but it's fine and handy for breaking the coals!"' Duggie wouldn't tell a lie."

"Not much," I said. "He was a sailor, wasn't he! What about the story he told us in the Breadalbane Arms, in Aberfeldy. About a bloke called MacBain who put on a bet about ghosts."

"Oh, I remember that one right enough," said Mull. "I'll tell it to you lads. Duggie with some mates who were working with him, were in this pub one winter's evening, and they were well shot, as they had been to the funeral of some old workmate who died, and was buried in the local cemetery. The landlord was drinking with them, as he had been to the funeral too.

"The crack eventually got round to ghosts, loneliness, and graveyards, when this bloke called MacBain maintained it was all baloney, and that he was afraid of nothing atall, alive or dead. So somebody put a bet on with him, that he wouldn't go up to the graveyard, with a sword that was hanging behind the bar, and stick it down to the hilt in the new grave. It was a bloody long sword, nearly as big as Willy Wallace's, that's hanging in yon monument of his in Stirling, and that's about five feet. MacBain accepted the bet, so away he staggered with the sword, out into the stormy night. The conditions of the bet was that the sword was to be left there until it was pulled out in the morning, by the landlord, sure they were all drunk.

"What happened next nobody really knows, but Mac was found on top of the grave next morning, as dead as a doornail. What they assumed to have happened, was that after he stuck the sword in the grave, he couldn't get away. God knows he tried, by the mess he made on top of the grave. The fright of being held, was too much for the heart, so he snuffed it.

"What really happened, by Duggie's account, when he pushed the sword down into the grave, he shoved it through the corner of his old overcoat, so he pinned himself to the grave. Of course he thought it was the playboy below that was holding on to him, and he croaked with fright."

"I'm damned if I'll believe that one either," said Ryan. "Talk about Malone, he wouldn't hold a candle to you lot. Holy japers do any of you ever go to confessions atall?"

"Nobody asked you to believe it," said Mull. "As for confessions, when you went there last, and the priest asked you to say the confiteor, you asked him to whistle the first of it."

"I would not like to be the poor priest who had to listen to Mull," said Ginger. "He would have grey hairs by the time he finished, or perhaps like the potential suicide wallah telling the remonstrating priest his problems, resulted in both of them jumping in the river."

"I knew a man back in Ireland," said Ryan, who went to confessions, and was kept waiting in the box for about ten minutes before he ventured to pull back the shutter to see if the priest was there. At that moment, Murphy the local shopkeeper who was in the opposite box did the very same thing, so they were both looking at one another across an empty chair. 'Where has the priest gone?' Murphy asked. Our man, who didn't like Murphy very much, answered, 'By cripes he must have gone for the police.'"

"I wouldn't blame him if he did, for shopkeepers are among the biggest rogues on earth," said Ryan. "On my oath, I witnessed one shopkeeper, back in my hometown of Newcastle in the hard old days, cutting a slice off a loaf o' bread because the wee boy who was buying it was a halfpenny short of the price. A loaf cost four pence halfpenny then."

"It is very hard to justify the likes of that," I said, "unless his mother was making a habit of being short—a halfpenny was a lot of money then. People don't believe that nowadays, they think you are talking about generations ago, and not living memory."

"I knew a man that jacked, over a halfpenny," said Ginger. "It was the principle of it, he said, and I agreed with him, you won't get served if you are a penny short, and that's today."

"Sure times were hard in those days, and large families were brought up on practically nothing," said Tinen. "Here in England as well as everywhere else. Lots of people think because they got it hard in their own countries, that all the people on this side of the water were living in the lap of luxury. If you ask me, in the knowledge that I've gained on my tramping, they were worse off here than anywhere, in the cities, I mean."

"I doubt that," said Ryan.

"Well you listen, Mick," I said. "I once worked with a lad who hailed from York, and in a similar discussion to this he made the following statement: 'You Pat, never knew what poverty was and be thankful, you always had a clean bed to go to, granted it might be raggy, but it was clean. You lived in a whitewashed cottage. Lime is a disinfectant. Food no doubt was scarce, but that was common, perhaps you may have lived on potatoes alone. I don't know, but you always had a drop of milk to drink, if not tea. That my friend is not poverty. Poverty is living in slums among rats, mice, and diseases, with rotten garbage lying around the back doors, and closets. Going into a tatty bed, lousy with fleas and nits, which no amount of washing could cure, bugs lurking behind the wallpaper, waiting for you. The food was every bit as scarce as yours but poorer in quality, picked up on cheap market stalls, by poor mothers who were striving to do their best for you on what few coppers they had. Often or not, asking the fishmonger for a bit of gash fish for the cat, I knew who the cat was. My dad, like many more dads, that was poverty, Pat. That's what overthrew governments, and bred hard union men. That was the breeding ground for communism.' So you can see that man's point, Mick, and he had done time for thieving, which he never considered to be a sin."

"I never looked at it that way," said Ryan thoughtfully. "He was right too, and there is stealing and stealing."

"Of course he was right," said Mull, "and what he said was true of every city, be it London, Dublin, Glasgow, or Cardiff. A Geordie lad told me about a woman in his street who used to buy two eggs daily—you could buy anything single then. One egg was for the old man's breakfast, the other was for the family, and there were five of them going to school. She used to line them all up in a row, and then go along the ranks with the boiled egg, smearing it on their lips, so as to leave a yoke stain. Then threaten hell on them if they rubbed it off. This was to make the neighbours think they all had an egg for breakfast."

"Go to blazes," said Ryan. "You are as bad as Malone, who maintained his father used to line the nine of them up in a row in front of the house with a slice of bread in their hands. Then he would let the old pig out, and belt hell out of him round and round the house, until he broke into a sweat. Then he would roar at the youngsters to get ready and wipe their slice on his back in the passing, bread and fresh dripping. Your story is worse than that."

Nobody could say much for laughing. I managed to get a round in.

"Things were indeed hard if not funny by times," said Mull. "I suppose like everything else, when passed you remember the good parts and try to forget the bad, as Pat said about the war. I remember a woman, back where my father came from, who had a pair of nippers, and a daughter. The nippers were about seven, and nine, but the daughter was a lovely eighteen. Now it came to pass, as the good book says, that she met this fine young English gent who took a fancy to her, and went courting her. After she realised he was getting a bit serious, she told the owld one, who told her in turn, to invite him round for tea.

"It was done, and everything was set, top-notch. The best china was out, by that I mean the cups that weren't cracked, and a tablecloth put on the table. The owld one, forever watching points, had chased the two young whelps away to bed, down to the room, and told to behave—that or a warm arse.

"However when the party was at its height, and the owld one making small talk, as she sipping her tea instead of gulping it, there came a shout from the room: 'Mother! Charlie is pulling the coat of the bed.'

"'Excuse me,' said herself through gritted teeth, as she rose and made for the room, making sure the door shut behind her. The cowering pair in the bed got the promised thumping, with a sound telling off. 'Do you want to shame me? There is no coat on the bed, it's a blanket, do you hear.' The pair nodded, their eyes peeping over the top. 'Blanket do you hear, and if I hear one more word out of you, I'll trim the living daylights out of you.' Then she returned to the living room, all smiles, saying boys will be boys, no doubt the teeth were still gritting. Things were back on a nice even keel again, until it was shattered once more, by a sudden roar from the room: 'Mother!' 'Yes, John, what is it?' she answered, showing polite surprise. 'Charlie has pulled the sleeve off the blanket.'

"That fluked that setup."

After a few minutes when Ryan managed to pull himself together, he seemed to pray. "What have I done on you God to deserve this. Sure I've sinned, God, but not to the extent of having to suffer this kind of punishment."

"Mull is just getting his own back on you, for all the punishment you dished out to him," said Tinen.

"The rain has stopped," I ventured to remark, hoping to change the subject for the sake of my sides.

Mull got up, went to the door, and looked out. "It is only taking a breather," he said, as he returned to the table. "It will be on again in a matter of minutes."

There were a few minutes of silence.

"That man over there," said Ryan, nodding towards a man at a corner table. "He has a glass eye."

"What about it," asked Mull. "Lots of people have a glass eye. How do you know it's a glass eye. It could be made of anything."

"It has to be glass. How else could he see through it?"

"There are some smart guys around here without a doubt."

"There is something I would like to know," asked Tinen. "Why did the tramp Malone always wear an earring?"

"Well," I said. "There are various reasons given, Tom. Some say it is good for arthritis, and so on, but the most authentic reason is the solid fact that while you are wearing anything gold, you are never broke. Apparently in the old days, and perhaps still the case, you could be had for vagrancy if caught penniless. Vagrancy was a very serious charge indeed, and therefore people of the open road—gypsies, tinkers, tramps, and navvies—took to carrying something of value on their person. So what was easier to carry than an earring or ring. Any manual worker with any brains knows not to wear a ring, unless he wants to lose a finger, so the navvy wore the earring. Some had a large gold ring through which they pulled the two corners of their neckchief instead, thus making a knot unnecessary, but that was easy to lose or steal."

"Did you ever notice how the gypsy women carry their wealth in rings," said Mull. "Just as the Chinese men carry it in gold teeth. Which reminds me of something Mike Sweeney told me a while back. Mike always hangs around that spike in the Mile End area of East London, which is near the docks.

"This concerns a Chinese, who was found by a copper sitting in the middle of Commercial Road one dark evening, his mouth covered in blood, and crying his eyes out. The copper couldn't make head nor tail of him, as he couldn't understand Chinese, so thinking he had been beaten up, he asked a passing seaman if he could help. He could. The seaman got through to him after a while, and then explained to the policeman. It seemed the Chinese man was going along the street after leaving his ship, when he saw this door with a red light over it, and though he knew no English, he thought he knew what a red light was for. So thinking it was something it wasn't, he went in. Thus he ended up in the middle of Commercial Road without a tooth in his head. Eastenders don't miss much."

"The Goldtooth O'Hanlon had a gold tooth, that's how he got the name," said Tinen. "I often wondered why he ever had it fixed in, for he was a marked man, no matter where he went. Somebody said he had been to America in his young days—perhaps it was there he got it done as a security for the future."

"I don't know about where he got it put in, but I know where he damn near got it knocked out," said Mull. "Whoever fixed it didn't skimp on the cement. He was one evening in the Throne bar in Edinburgh, showing the landlord how to drink a pint without using your hands. There he was with his two hands clamped behind his back, bent over the counter with a pint pot gripped in his teeth, and drinking the beer, when in the door came the Moocher Dogherty. Seeing the Hanlon in the predicament he was in, he couldn't resist giving him a mighty thump between the shoulder blades as he shouted, 'Howdo Goldie!' Goldtooth's chin and pot hit the counter with a clatter that made smithereens of the pot, and blasted Goldtooth's breath out through his nose, like an angry bull, with such force that he smothered the landlord in beer. When Goldtooth got his breath back he drew a wallop on the Moocher that stretched him full length on the floor. The landlord, having wiped himself down, was now rearing to go. He didn't make for the root of the trouble atall, but for poor Goldtooth, grabbing him by the scuff of the neck, and the slack arse of his trousers, he railroaded him through the door at about sixty miles an hour without even bothering to open it. Then he came back looking for the Moocher, but the Moocher was an old campaigner, and already on the move snaking along the wall behind the landlord's back, and was clear away before he could be caught. But as he bolted out the door he shot straight into Goldtooth's swinging fist, for he had worked out his estimate time of arrival. Two coppers watching this performance were on their toes, and frogmarched the pair away, leaving a trail of bloody spits from two broken mouths."

"The Moocher was an evil bugger," said Ginger. "Never moved far from that kip in the Grassmarket. I was there one day when rumour came round that he had won a lab on the horses, and mind you there were a few rubbing their hands in anticipation as the Moocher, regardless of other things, was not mean. His arrival at the kip was greeted like royalty, but that soon petered out when it became clear that the old suitcase he was carrying was his own. I like the rest thought he had bought himself some new gear. Not on your blooming life. When he opened the case, there on display was the finest collection of screwtop beer bottles I ever saw. Talk about herring in a box, they couldn't have been better packed. Everyone got drunk, including the deputy, who had to be carried to bed, being an old man. Next morning everything was back to square one. Dogherty on the mooch again."

"He wouldn't waste good drinking money on gear if he could help it atall," said Tinen. "Blowing about how much he spent while mooching at the same time was his carry on. He could work when he wanted to, though, but a very excitable man. Cripes, when he saw the foreman coming it was not safe to be near him. Once when working behind the mixer with him I happened to remark that the GF was coming. Holy Moses man, he split the bag of cement on my back, before I had a chance to drop it in the hopper. I damn near took the shovel to him.

"Himself and a Polish fellow were sent to erect one of them collapsible canvas shelters one day. Granted they are not easy to erect, just like one of them chairs you see at the seaside. The Pole was a cranky bugger, and did not like the Moocher. The feeling was mutual. However they were getting themselves into a terrible tangle as it was a gusty day. The Moocher was calm enough, his way was Jack Sampie's way: 'Take plenty no notice.' The Pole was getting madder and madder, ranting away in a mixture of English and Polish, with 'Paddy bloody stupid' coming out here and there. At long last they managed to get it into some kind of shape, and the Pole went inside to lock the rib stiffners. Whatever the Moocher done outside, it was something he shouldn't have done, perhaps he misunderstood the Pole's muttering through the canvas, but the whole shamoodle collapsed like a house of cards on top of the Pole. The Moocher knowing he would annihilate him once he got out, decided not to give him that chance, and getting in there first, he grabbed a shovel, and laid into the canvas heap—everywhere he saw a moving lump, he let fly with the shovel. The more the Pole struggled and raged, the more bumps he made, so the more thumps he got. Whether he was finally knocked out or not, he stopped struggling long enough for the Moocher to make his getaway. They never met again, because the Moocher is still alive and kicking around Edinburgh."

"The Moocher was God's gift to some poor woman," said Ryan. "I suppose she watched him grow up, thinking he might be another Finn McCool or the president of Ireland, instead of that he ends up mooching in Edinburgh."

I said, "I suppose all the clousters whom we knew in our time earned their nicknames in some strange way. Strangely one can remember a nickname easier than you do the right one."

"What's the weather doing?" asked Ryan of Ginger, who just returned from being outside placing a bet.

"It has turned to sleet with the ground all slushy. I think it will end up raining, if it doesn't start freezing. Still anything is better than show."

"I don't think this rain will ever cease by the looks of it," said Mull through clenched teeth, as they were gripping his pipe. "This bloody town is getting as bad as Manchester for rain. Like the tale about a fellow who got himself killed in a trench, and went to the waiting room at the pearly gates, where he was given the customary little job to do, pending a decision on his misdemeanours down below. A sort of probation. After a few days he asked to be sent to hell, as he found the work too hard. His job? Up and down to Manchester with rain."

"I don't doubt it," I agreed. "It would drive anybody to hell, though Mancunians don't take well to that crack, even though they probably started it themselves, like the Aberdonian and his meanness."

"I wonder where all those yarns come from," mused Ryan. "More than likely there is a smattering of truth in most of them, just unusual occurrences turned around, with a bit added."

"I would say more than a smattering," I added, "for I have heard stories years ago, about things that actually happened, and indeed I have witnessed the funniest of occurrences in the remotest of places, things you would not credit. Only to hear them related on the radio, years later. Mind you, twisted out of all proportion. I'll tell you something else. If you are knocking around Shepherd's Bush in London, watch what you say, for there's where those scriptwriters hang around, with their ears cocked, waiting to pick up any morsel of value that can be cleverly twisted to suit their ends."

"Ach! Sure when you go to Ireland nowadays, the place is alive with them," said Young Bob. "They are in every pub, seated away in a corner, looking like hikers, with a pad inside the folded map, jotting down the old boys' crack. After all it's their bread and butter, and sure it makes pleasant listening, better recorded than lost forever."

"By crikey you are right too, young fellow," I said. "These old boys had a wit, if nothing else. They could cut you, or each other, to the bone. Reminds me of a wit who used to knock around this country, by the name of Darkie, as sharp as a lance. He was once working outside Nottingham, during the war years, when labour was controlled. In other words, you couldn't jack. But don't think you got away with murder, far from it. You were suspended for a number of days according to your misdemeanour, which meant losing money. This Tuesday the Darkie was up in front of the personnel officer for missing Monday, a serious crime when working a seven-day week, any day bar Monday. 'Where were you yesterday?' he was asked. 'I had to wash my shirt.' 'You could have sent it to the laundry.' 'If I did that I'd have to miss a week.'

"The Darkie got away with it, when no one else would."

"There were many tales about him," said Tinen. "The one I liked best concerned the time he was sent to Scunthorpe on a cable job. There was a drop of water in the trench, which was more of a nuisance than anything. The old gangerman was one of those types that keep their toeplates over-hanging the edge of the trench all day. 'One would think you would put a sod of some kind in front of that water, and not have it following you all day,' he grunted at Darkie. Darkie looked at the water for a while, then looked up at the grunter. 'It will have a job following me, for I intend to be in Camden Town tonight.' Which he was."

"Cable men would not be easy found around Scunthorpe, I should think," said Mull. "But mentioning Camden Town reminds me of an evening long ago, while sitting in the Brighton. A runt of a young fellow at the bar was jabbering away as if he had been around for years—in fact he had only just arrived, and just finished his first shift. 'I always thought you worked hard in this country,' said he. 'Baloney! You don't know what a hard day's work is. The hardest day's work I ever did, was a day's ploughing, back in Ireland.'

"Old Dan O'Brien was sitting with me on the wall bench, puffing away on his pipe, with one knee crossed over the other to make an elbow rest for his pipe arm. He just looked at him for a while before he spoke. 'Young man,' he said, 'I suppose it depends on which end of the plough you were on.' Dan spoke but seldom."

"Another funny bugger I met on my travels was the May Morning," said Tinen. "I remember working with him on a farm near Carstairs once. I'm damned if I rightly know what took me there in the first place, for I was never a lover of farmers. The May always spent what he termed his 'summer vacation on the agriculture side of the fence'. Good honest food, and well away from cement stour, he always maintained. During the war years, lots of young fellows got lost among the farmers, to avoid being called up for military service. One could get by there, without the normal documentations required, as long as you kept your nose clean. Some local authorities turned a blind eye, as you were doing work of national importance anyway, and were helping out a local friend. The farmer gave you what was known as a bothy to stay in. In other words, a little one-room house near the farmhouse, where you fended for yourself, just getting milk, and perhaps a bit of butter and cheese from the farmer's wife, potatoes and vegetables were plentiful. In a way you were self-employed, no cards, no stamps, and no hassle. It was ideal if you liked that kind of life, or handy if on the run.

"Mind you one had to be a good at stealing hens too, that's if you liked a bit of meat now and again, of course you never shit on his own doorstep, if you know what I mean. A few ill-gotten eggs also came in handy, to barter in some city pub, when you were in the know. I knew a chap who kept the village bobby in eggs for the duration. The bobby never questioned where he came from, or why was he not out fighting, and he was never conscripted.

"I was not that lucky, for they hauled me out of bed one morning, and stuck a uniform on me. Pat here was the same, but unluckier still, for they shoved him up the jungles of Burma for a spell. In the latter years you could opt for the coal pits instead of the armed services. They were known as the Bevin Boys."

"Damn me it was rough enough," said Ryan. "I was damn near caught myself, but I got away because I could prove I was not here the two years specified, before they could grab you. It must have been rough in the Far East, Pat."

"Ach! You only remember the good times. I think there is some built-in mechanism in the mind that arranges that, it wasn't me that was there, some other person. I was luckier than most, as I was on the water. Not a lot of cover, but at least a chance to see your enemies. However I came home, while thousands didn't."

"Died for damn all," said Ginger.

"Oh, I wouldn't say that," said Mull. "Somebody had to stop the Nazis, and the Japanese, those men gave their all. It's some of today's morons that discredit their cause. I'm not talking of the regular soldier, who joins the army for a living. I'm talking of the man that laid down the plough for the sake of his people and his principles, done a job, and if lucky, went back to his plough."

"The May Morning was over the hill for conscription when you were with him, Tom," I said, just to change the subject.

"Oh, he was indeed, but he was in the first lot right enough. What he done there I couldn't say, no doubt as little as possible. Though I did hear he was with the gravedigging mob.

"However, as we are on about him, I'll tell you a tale he told me while on yon farm I mentioned earlier. Apparently he was tramping from Edinburgh to Glasgow one time, and garbed in the navvy's regalia of the day. Drum hooked on the trouser belt, small kitbag over the shoulder tied with a string to the galluses' buckle, and the knife and spoon in the breast pocket. The drum was the standard model, a burned-black syrup tin with a handle added.

"'Well Tam,' he said to me, 'I was tramping away like a good one, making good headway, as the weather was good, and the road was quiet. I was planning on making a Glasgow model lodging house before nightfall. Suddenly I felt a bit hungry as my thoughts turned to a cob of bread and some cheese in my bag, so all I needed was something to wash it down with. I was thinking of making a fire, when I spied this ploughman's house along the road. You could always tell the farm workers' cottages, as they were generally near the road, with their backs to it. This gave them a bit of privacy, while convenient for travelling shops. It also protected the children from passing traffic. Now most ploughmen's wives are the salt of the earth. None more generous to the needy, but damn me man, the article that answered yon door to me, was everything but. "Could you spare me a wee drop of hot water ma'am?" I asked, offering her the drum. Now that was not a lot to ask for. She grabbed it out o' my hand with a shout. "I'm sick and tired of tramps begging at my door. There is plenty water in the ditch along the road there, which is good enough for your kind." Well I'll be buggered, I thought to myself, but to hell! I might as well hang for a sheep a lamb, so I'll tap her for a drop o' milk. Which I did.

"'She grabbed hold of the edge of the door with both hands, for a minute I thought she meant to lift it off its hinges and clout me with it, for she was big enough. "Get to hell before I call the police," she spat, as she slammed it in my face. Ah well, nothing ventured nothing gained, I thought, as I added my wee grain of tea to the water before it went cold. Now as you know yourself, you have to swing a drum over your head to mix tea. Well I was just doing that as I passed along the side of the house when, great balls of fire man! didn't the damn handle come away from the drum, and off went the bloody thing through her bedroom window, making smithereens of the pane. What damage it did inside I didn't wait to see, for on the first screech from within I was off. Now didn't I make the second-biggest mistake of my life, a novice wouldn't do it. I kept to the road. Half a mile away they caught me. I was taken to Peebles Police Station, and charged with begging, willful damage to property, and losing control of my drum. I got fourteen days.

"'By japers I always made sure I used good strong bullwire for drum handles after that. But sure it was her fault for snatching it from me in the first instance—weakened the handle. That plea fell on deaf ears in the courthouse. Apparently, a dim view is taken of anybody losing control of his drum.'"

"The same bugger could tell them," said Ryan. "Though no doubt it happened to him. I've seen many a drum go flying off the handle when being swung, and a few narrow escapes from being badly scalded too, at the same caper.

"Ned Boyle was telling me that he and the May went to Lanark looking for work once. There was a market in Lanark every Monday morning, and it was there you would find all the local farmers. Most of the men looking for work knew all the farmers, and the farmers knew them. The May and Ned having scrounged their fares in Glasgow, had arrived there bright and early, as it was November time, and one had to be lively to get any work. They were weighing up points when the May spotted a farmer he had worked for on numerous occasions, and had left with a clean slate. Not always the case. So he approached him. 'Good morning, Mr Crawford.' 'Oh, good morning May. How are ye getting on?' replied Mr Crawford. 'Oh, I've been about a bit, here and there as one might say. Have you got anything doing Mr Crawford?' 'Nay, nay, man, all ma work is tidied up the noo. Can ye come back in the spring?' 'Spring! Spring! What do you think I am, the bloody cuckoo!' said the May, as he turned on his heels."

"Oh, like him," laughed Tinen. "But the Boyle himself wasn't slow with his answers. We were also on a farm during the war, draining a field, and hard ground it was too. However, the old farmer was keen to get on with his ploughing, and offered us an extra bonus if we could finish at a certain time, which we did, and he was highly delighted, so pleased that he asked us into the house for a dram, while he paid us.

"We went in, and he paid up like a good un. Then he went to a wall cupboard that was built like a safe, and produced a square whiskey bottle, smothered in cobwebs. We watched him as he reverently poured out three drams. 'Aye, aye,' said he, as he inspected his glass through the window light. 'Would ye believe me, that whiskey is a hundred years auld.' Ned was now looking at his dram through the light as well. 'Mon,' said he, imitating the farmer's accent, as he shook his head, 'isn't it sma' for its age.'

"The old farmer never let on he heard him, just drank our health, and wished us well as we left."

"Boyle was witty, and no doubt," said Mull, after he came back with the beer. "We were once in digs together, with this old thing in Glasgow. She reared up on him one night because he complained about the dinner she shoved in front of him. I had already rejected the same dinner, and had told her that I was off, so she was now giving vent to her frustration on Boyle. The bloody dinner wasn't fit for a dog, giblets from some old vulture that died of the clap or something, in Glasgow zoo where her husband worked.

That's what Boyle thought, and said as much. 'Get out!' she roared. 'Get to hell you Irish pig. You came here without a halfpenny in your pocket, and now you tell me my dinner is not good enough for you. Get out.'

"'I know I didn't have a lot in my pockets when I came here,' replied Boyle, 'but I had pockets, which is more than you had, for you came here stark bloody naked.' She flung a plate after him as he dived for the door."

"Some landladies were terrible," mused Ginger, shaking his head. "I'm just thinking of the Long Dogherty and Greenie, when they were staying with a bad one in Middlesbrough. She was a bad feeder too. Greenie was telling me the crack about what happened. It seems they were all sitting in the living room, her and the old fellow by the fire, and the pair of lodger at the table, after finishing their bit of dinner, when a puff of gas escaping from one of the embers made a hole in the ashes. 'Oh look,' she remarked. 'There is a hole in the ashes, where I come from that means there's a stranger coming to the house.' 'Could be the butcher,' said Dogherty, nice and quiet. Greenie reckoned he just came out with it without thinking, however they had to go, which was no great loss."

"There are quite a few stories told about landladies, but for every bad one there was also a good one. Couldn't do enough for you," I said. "I have met some of the best along with the worst on my travels—you must remember some lodgers could never be pleased. I knew one who complained one morning that his egg was the wrong way up in the cup. Such characters are about, you know."

Tinen had just returned to the table. "You know what I was thinking while in the toilets there," he remarked. "The Putlog McBride was as witty a man as I ever met on my travels, though he was unaware of it himself. We all know he was an annoying bugger, but he was also funny."

"You can say that again," I agreed. "Often I wondered how he didn't get his head knocked off sometimes, for he had the knack of saying the wrong thing at the wrong time, be it sarcastic or funny, he could be damn stupid too. A funny tale I heard about him, concerning a job he took on one time, as a drainlayer, something he could never do, for he was useless at whatever he tried, with the exception of scaffolding for bricklayers, hence the nickname.

"He managed to lay a reasonable line of pipes between a pair of man-holes, but then came the tricky part, the jointing. Yarn and compo jointing is not an amateur's crack, but he had a go anyway. When the clerk of works came along on the following midday to give them the usual water test, he condemned the lot, for the water was pissing out at every joint. Needless to say the Putlog was condemned in turn by the gangerman.

"So later on we find him sitting alone in the nearest inn, enjoying a pint of the best, with the daily paper open in front of him, as he studied the nags. It was a beautiful summer's day, with all doors and windows wide open, and the cricket season at its full height. England against Australia, at Lord's. The bar radio was tuned in of course, as it was the topic of the day among Englishmen. The brave Putlog was just about to mark out his sure thing for the two thirty at Haydock, when he was interrupted by this character that slipped in from the other bar, nursing a glass of some pink stuff, and sporting a cream pullover with a paisley cravat. 'I say old chap, how goes the jolly-old test, as I have just arrived. What ho!' he asked, as he cocked a well-manicured ear to the radio behind the bar.

"The Putlog looked up dumbfounded, then looked around the bar. It was a while before he managed to stutter, 'Fucking useless, they wouldn't hold broken bricks.' Our man just stood there for a minute staring at him, before he shuffled back to where he came from, and ordering a large one, of the pink stuff. No doubt to ponder over what kind of people were building workers. Sure the Putlog knew as much about cricket as he did about pipe jointing."

We enjoyed that crack, and smiled as our sympathy went to the poor fellow who had to come across the Putlog.

"Does anybody know what happened to him atall? Is he alive or dead?" asked Mull.

"Dead! Not bloody likely," answered Tinen. "He is very much alive and kicking indeed, around Newcastle, on the opencast coalfields, doing his timber man. Someone told me he was living over the sticks with some squaw. The Slew McGinty is along with him."

"When a man takes in the squaw, he's done for," muttered Ryan.

"So that's where he is," I mused. "Along the Slew, a fine pair to wish on any town. I once worked with the Slew, up in Scotland, he seldom left there in his young days. I never heard of him being at the timbering, though, must have picked up what he needed, in and around Newcastle. I'm damn sure he learned nothing from the Putlog for it would be a case of the blind leading the blind. I'm surprised they haven't killed each other by now."

"Well that's what they are at," said Tinen. "Though I don't think there is much tricky work attached to opencast coal work, as most of that excavation is battered, it will be just bits and pieces no doubt."

"Myself and a man called Tim Bonner were making for the Glencoe Bar in Falkirk one day," I said. "We were running as it was pouring down, and we had just been rained off for the day, and as we neared the pub door, who should jump out in front of us but the Slew. 'You couldn't see your way to lend me ten bob, until I straighten myself out, Tim?' he asked. The bloody moocher knew better than to ask me. 'Fuck off!' roared Tim. 'It would take a fluking steamroller to straighten you out.'"

"Some people called him the Moocher instead of Slew," said Tinen. "I know fine he could work, for he was in yon camp up in Glen More, and on that tunnel in Glen Affric too."

"Of course he was, and was chased for mooching around the camp, sure he was making a fortune from the boys that didn't know him there, but by cripes they soon did. Big Yorkie the grouter was the man for him. One night in the wet-canteen Yorkie asked him how long had he the slew. 'Since I was a boy, I was kicked by a horse,' his usual tale. The nearest he ever came to anything resembling a horse was perhaps when he had a nightmare. 'Tha never tried to do nought about it?' 'Oh! my father spent thousands trying to fix it,' lied the Slew. 'Well,' said Yorkie. 'I'll soon fix it for thee. In fact ah might slew it t'other way, if tha don't stop talking about me round camp.'"

"By dad, that would frighten anybody so it would, the size of Yorkie," said Tinen. "He was a mountain of a man to be sure. The Slew was a bugger for talking behind people's backs, so he must have said something derogatory about him that got back to him. Yorkie was not one to panic for he was like a big teddy bear."

Our eyes now turned to the door as Big John McCarthy, one of the banksmen, made his entrance. He was like a wet hen, soaked to the skin. As he passed, Mull gave him money to get a drink. On his return from the bar he took the offered chair as he wiped his face with his cap.

"Fuck the snow and the sleet," he muttered with emphasis. "Bloody agent told me he would book me the whole day if I ran a message for him, asked me to nip into town, and deliver a letter to the architect's office. I had to walk all the way there and back. Them buses are cat, when it's wet."

"If they want you to be a postie, then they should give you a cap—one of the kind posties wear, with a glazed peak. I'm thinking it might suit you too," grinned Ryan.

"Piss off," said Mac, as he took a long slug from his pint. "Didn't I hear someone mention the Slew, as I came in?"

"We were just talking about him sure enough," I answered. "Have no fear, he is not around, as he is in Newcastle working. Why, did you know him?"

"That is no way far enough," he replied. "It's out in the North Sea he should be, just to make sure he don't come back. Did I know him. He owes me a fiver. Still worse, was a mate he had up in Inveraray, the Slew Carrol. Yes, another one. One beetle knows another one, as my father always said. Nobody takes a blind bit of notice of a man with a bit of a deformity, but that pair of bastards were good for nothing. When you seen the pair of them together in the wet-canteen, it was time to look out. Both heads nearly touching as they bumped shoulders while leaning on the bar. Tim Bonner once remarked, 'Look at them, both brought up in the one bell tent.' There was a story going about, that Slew McGinty went to visit a mate of his who was in hospital after getting hurt, no doubt the object was to do a bit of scrounging, seeing as the mate was in dry dock and unable to spend, he might help him out by doing it for him. However, while he waited for a bus outside the hospital, after the visiting time, a well-dressed gent approached him, and asked very politely, 'Excuse me, but how long has your head been that way?' The Slew weighed him up for a while before answering, to make sure perhaps that he was not another Yorkie. He decided not. 'Since I was a little boy, I got kicked by a horse.' Somebody back in the queue who obviously knew him, got an almighty fit of coughing. 'I am a surgeon who specialises in those kind of things,' said the gent. 'Twisted bones and ligaments, which includes kinky necks. So here's my card, perhaps you could call and see me sometime.' He must have been a smart man.

"Now it is said, the Slew did go to see him, and spent a week in hospital, before marching out as straight as a guardsman. Lourdes couldn't have made a better job on him. He marched straight into a local pub, and ordered a large scotch. Incidentally, he was barred in the same house, but sure they didn't know him now. The Slew smiled to himself as he raised the drink, and threw it back. Hell man, instead of going down the hatch, the bloody lot went straight over his shoulder! He was thunderstruck, and shook to ribbons, so he ordered another one. The same thing, straight over the shoulder it went. That was it! Enough for the Slew. Straight back to the hospital he went, and told the doctor, 'Put my mouth back where it was.' So he will remain the Slew until somebody hangs him."

After the laughter died, I managed to remark, "I wouldn't doubt it atall for I never saw anybody knock it back like him. A drop of spirits never touched that man's lips since he took his first one, it was his tonsils that took the strain. How any man can drink like that, beats me, you should savour your drink, just as you would a good-looking woman."

"Thanks God the Slew never touched the women," laughed Mull. "But a while ago when we were talking about the Putlog, and his attempt at the pipe-laying crack, reminds me of a similar fellow by the name of Kilday, who would have a go at anything reasonable. I'll tell you about one of his exploits. When McAlpine was doing the Port Talbot Steelworks in South Wales, he landed on site looking for the start. As he was not known to anybody there, he couldn't get fixed up atall, every section gave the standard answer, 'Full up,' until somebody told him they were looking for a blacksmith in the black gang. That was enough for the dauntless Kilday, so away he went to see the steam boss, who started him right away when he told him he had worked in his father's forge, back in Ireland.

"That same boss was a man I knew well, and one of the best in the game. So I was not surprised to hear that the first thing he wanted Kilday to make was a seven-pound hammerhead. That to any blacksmith is a tough task. In fact I never heard of one making such a thing. However Kilday was not to be beaten, for he nipped out the gate to the nearest iron-monger's, and bought one. Getting back, he threw it in the fire, heatened it up, and knocked hell out of it, especially round the maker's stamp. After cooling it in the water tank, it looked the real McCoy, so, well satisfied with his work, he threw it on the floor. Oh, he had the old blacksmith's tricks off to a tee.

"When the steam boss came back after breakfast, he found the hammerhead where he expected to find it, on the floor among the dirth. As he examined it, Kilday pretended to be interested in something else, though he was watching the boss man out of the corner of his eye.

"'That's a good job,' said the boss, as he turned it around in his hand. 'Aye, a damn good job. I want you to make me two dozen of them now, like a good man.' That was the end of that crack. Kilday had to go, so you see the Putlog was not alone in being a chancer."

"Cripes, he had a nerve," said Tinen. "If it were today now, and he could do a bit of burning, and welding, he might have managed to get away with it for a spell, but in those days, not the hope of a snowball in hell! Anyway fair play to him for trying, a pity he came unstuck."

"We will become unstuck if we don't make a move, as the bell is gone," said Ginger.

"Give us time to drink up. You are not talking to the Slew," said Ryan.

"Right then," said Mull, as he rose. "Who is going my way?"

"I am," I said, as I joined him, and with a cheerio here and there we left the pub. The sleet had turned to rain as Ginger had predicted, which cheered us up, for who wants snow!

Chapter 6

Christmas was only a week away, and it had all the appearances of being a white one. Today it was raining, very cold rain that could easily turn into sleet or snow, very quickly indeed. The sky above the moors had been dull and overcast over the last few days, with a northeastern wind that would cut you in two. We knew something was in the offings, and today confirmed it. The job was closed down at breakfast time, and that was that. We were rained off for the day.

We were now gathered in the Brown Cow in Ripende, having a few jars, while the reservoir we were constructing lay deserted, and glittering in the wet, above on the moors, about two miles away. As far as we were concerned it didn't exist, not until Monday morning anyway, for today was Friday. The day the cow calves. Payday, in other words.

The Brown Cow was a very cosy little house, ran by two old ladies, who really enjoyed doing so, and it showed, by their pleasantness. Not the commercial pleasantness of town houses, of landlords whose only real pleasure is the constant ringing of the till. If any of them ever kneeled in prayer to the sound of a bell, it would be to that of the till.

Pat Roarty, Tom Tinen, Brian Larkin, Ryan, and myself were seated at a table under the small window that looked out over the valley below. On a sunny day you could see for miles. Even the tall chimney stacks of the mill at Sowerby Bridge. A lovely view, but hidden today under a curtain of rain.

Away at the far end of the house, beyond the standing drinkers, a huge coal fire crackled. Tended to by a few old-timers that occupied the side benches. They were locals, and respected as of them, in fact when you went into the pub they changed gear, from English to their own lingo. The left-hand drive, Muldoon called it.

"Ach! you weren't there long enough to bless youself," said Ryan. "Old people are the same in most country places, just don't like you interloping on their domain. On the other hand some having found a stranger, will bore you to tears with their crackle. Danny Burk was telling me about a time when he was pea-picking at a place called Church Fenton. One midday he had to pack up because of the rain, and adjourn to the nearby Half Moon. On entering the bar, soaked to the skin, he ordered a pint and a whiskey, before making for the fire and try to dry himself out a little bit. There was an old sage seated there already, looking up the chimney, with a half-empty pint of mild on the hob. He stared at Danny from under the brim of an old straw hat, then suddenly gave vent to a 'Har!' from somewhere in his beard. It startled Danny, who was seated opposite him, but he paid no more notice. 'Har!' came the second bark. 'Har! Would tha believe that I am ninety-four years of age!' came the squeaky sound, like the constant creaking of a half-shut gate. Danny still ignored him, he had his own worries, as he held out his steaming trouser legs to the heat. 'Har! Does thou hear me, does tha believe me, that I'm ninety-four years of age. Har!' 'I would,' said Danny. 'I bloody would, and if you told me it was your second time around, I would believe that too.'"

"It will soon be Christmas," said Tinen, after a while. "Two week Saturday is Christmas Eve, damn me how time flies, it seems like only yesterday since it was last Christmas."

"Aye," added Ryan. "Monday for Boxing Day, and it's back to harness again on Tuesday. Somebody said that they are recognising Christmas as a holiday in Scotland now." He nodded over his shoulder towards Big Pat Roarty who had his back to us. "I know it was officially a holiday, but nobody paid much heed to it; it's about high time the heathens got up to date. Some missionary must have got through to them, some relations of Roarty's I'll be bound."

"Hold the fluking line there Ryan," said Roarty with emphasis, for he was a Glaswegian. "Just because it was not celebrated in Scotland don't make us out to be a pack of nonbelievers. Most Scots honour Christmas for what it is, a religious time, and New Year for what it is, a drinking time. Not like the hypocrites down south here that make Christmas a time for gluttony, and debauchery, not to mention sodomy. No bloody wonder most English women get a faraway look in their eye when they hear 'Christmas party' mentioned. You bloody Irish lot are worse still, as you just go to an extra Mass at Christmas, and New Year. Perhaps a jar or two after Mass, and a wee bit extra dinner, then, that's your bloody lot till next year."

"Oh," said Tinen. "We hung up our stockings when we were small too. Granted there weren't much around to put in them, perhaps an apple and an orange, but it was something. Damn it man, I used to keep that apple all day before eating it, for I knew once it was gone so was Christmas, until far off next year. It was a bit on the optimistic side getting up at the crack of dawn, to see what you got, and knowing full well it would be the same old apple again. Hope strives forever.

"It's not what you get that counts, it's the thoughts," said Ginger.

"Miracles can always happen," said Mull, as he pulled on his old pipe. "There was a whelp called McGarvie in my locality who was a proper tearaway, in spite of numerous thick ears, in fact I think he thrived on them. However the father told the mother to leave his stocking in his hands on this Christmas Eve, and that he would deal with him, he did. He filled it up with horse dung out in the stable, and then hung it back by the fire. Mind you the old girl was not too pleased about it atall.

"Anyway the story went, that next morning while the rest of the children were getting their apples and oranges out, a little sister asks our lad why was he rooting about in his stocking, and sending lumps of dung everywhere. 'Because there's a fluken horse in here somewhere,' he answered."

"Ach! Fluke off," laughed Tinen. "Though I did hear of a young fellow who had to spend a Christmas with his old grandfather, as his widowed mother had to go away somewhere on very urgent business. Some good neighbour reminded the old boy about putting something in the wee fellow's stocking on Christmas Eve. 'Oh, I've heard about that caper right enough, I'll see to it never mind,' he answered. However on Christmas morning after Mass the same neighbour collared the wee lad outside the chapel, and asked him if he got something nice in his stocking. 'Oh aye,' he said. 'I got an Easter egg.'"

"I suppose it was better than nothing," I said, as we all laughed. "What would that old clouster know about Santa Claus. I'm bloody sure he never came near him when he was young, and had he heard about him or enquired about him, as sure as hell it's a box in the ear he got. Maybe it was the best way. They make too much of such things nowadays. Motherdays, Fatherdays, birthdays. The whole salamander gets the treatment. Cripes I remember going along the road with my father when we met someone he knew, and after some chit chat he was asked which one of the brood was I. 'Oh, that's Paddy.' 'How old is he,' was the next question. 'Oh! I think he was seven sometime last month.' That was my birthdays for you!"

"Sure a lot of people around our age back beyond has nothing near the right dates on their birth certificates," said Tinen. "Simply because they were brought into the world by some old local woman who specialised in such crack. Baptised before they got a chance to object, just in case they croaked, as many of them did, and registered at leisure. That would be on the next visit to town, which could be anything up to a year.

"Now there was a law afoot that promised a hefty penalty for anyone not registering a birth or a death, within a certain number of days after the event. Elementary things like that were surmounted by simply bringing the date forward to coincide with the town visit, and also conform to the law. Then as the position of registrar was only a part-time job, the best place to collar him when needed was in his local pub. Details were generally scribbled on some handy scrap of paper to be entered in the book later, when sober. This left a further margin for error, depending on the state of the registrar and the whereabouts of the piece of paper, again that state was not improved on by the admission of an addition to one's family. Babies' heads have to be wetted.

"Another crack was the naming of a newborn after a deceased member of the family. One woman I knew was the third Nora in that house, the predecessors having been taken care of by the heavy child mortality of that time. I only found out when I heard she qualified for the pension six years before her time. The eldest Nora's certificate, you see. Cripes you couldn't be up to them."

"Ach! sure the half of them were not registered atall," said Ryan, as he lit his pipe, "and damn the bit difference it made. Just a bit extra rooting maybe, when claiming for the pension, that was the only time it was ever required. Marriage! Their word was good enough. That's why a good look at the teeth was advisable, before asking her, a bloody lot of them were a shade longer in the tooth than they ought to be. Sure everybody in this country were suppose to register at the outbreak of war, but did they? Not likely, a hell of a lot got by, in spite of all the regulations enforced. Myself included, and the governments knew it. If they thought they could get away with it, they would have everyone tattooed with a number, at birth. It might come yet."

"That reminds me," said Mull. "Do you remember James Brogan, Pat? He worked in Edinburgh with us."

"Indeed I do, the old bugger," I replied.

"Well he had a cousin of the same name married in Perth. Now listen till you hear this crack, lads, about the pair of them. The James in Perth, which for argument sake, we will call James the first, was celebrating the birth of his first born, when James the second turned up to give him a hand. Though the event occurred on the Friday, they were still at it on the Monday, when they had to make their way to the registry office to do the necessities, on the wife's demand, and none of them had been in such a place before. So I went with them.

"The pair were well cut, as one of them rung the little brass bell on that hallowed counter. A counter that must have taken the full harvest of a swarm of bees to polish. Like the genie of the lamp, a little man appeared behind it, and was now observing them over a pair of half-moon glasses. His two cheeks like a pair of ripe tomatoes, matched his nose.

"'Hem!' said he, as he cleared his throat. I half expected him to break into a chant of 'Does thou take ...' but he didn't. 'Aye you want tae register a birth I believe. Hem!' He pulled out a large leather-bound book, of the kind the old school master used when calling the roll long ago. Then he picked up a long quill pen, and opened the book.

"Now they tell me the Book of Kells is nice—well this book was a sight to behold. Beautiful copper plate writing of the finest quality, with a million wiggles and squiggles in decoration. There was a large sheet of blotting paper to be placed under the scribe's hands, to protect the scroll when writing.

"The old sage now seated himself on a high stool, fitted two white cardboard cuffs to his wrists, took control of the quill, dipped it in a large inkwell, and pushing his tongue out at the corner of his mouth, and asked, 'Name of the bairn?' 'Teresa, Mary,' answered Brogan number two, as Brogan number one was wrestling with a squashed box of matches. The old boy now bent to his labour. 'Ter … e … sa … Mar … y,' he intoned, as he squiggled the capitals, and the quill moved reverently across the hallow page. 'Your name?' he addressed James number two. 'James Brogan.' 'Ja … mes … Bro …gan,' went the chant, in keeping with the quill. 'Relations to the bairn? Father, I suppose.' 'Not bloody likely—he's the father,' said two, pointing at Brogan number one. Who, having solved the problem with the matchbox, now decided to count the change in his pocket.

"'Ach! Dearie, dearie me,' wailed the sage in despair. 'Dearie me. What have I deen? Fory years, and never a wrong letter in ma guid book, now I've gan and ruined it.' Nearly in tears he picked up a ruler, and drew a nice neat line through 'James Brogan'. I think he added a squiggle at each end, but I'm not sure. 'Come here you,' he called Brogan the first. 'Are you the father of this unfortunate baby?' 'I am, and less of the fucking unfortunate crack.' 'Nay, nay, I didna mean that, just a wee slip o the tongue. Ye ken, I'm sorry. I'm aw mixed up just noo, just bide there for a while until ah clean ma glasses. Now your name, please.' 'James Brogan.' 'Ja … mes … Bro … gan. Ach! Christ. I've deen it again. Ach! I'm sair destroyed, so I am.' He drew a mighty stroke through the second 'James Brogan'. No ruler now. He stood up, rubbed his eyes with his fists. I think he was counting or sobbing. When he picked up the quill again, he looked at Brogan number one. 'What is your name?' 'James Brogan.' 'Your name is James Brogan?' Then he looked at number two. 'What's your name then?' 'James Brogan.'

"The sage sat down very sudden, one elbow resting on the desk, as he wiped his forehead and bald head with a large red hankie. After a while he rose, a bit unsteady on it, and addressed them again. 'You'—to James the second—'take a wee seat over there, and dinna move. Now you'—to James the first—'come here, you are James Brogan , and the father.' 'I am that.'

"The old sage started again. Name. Relationship. Everything going fine until, occupation? 'Irish,' answered James the first. The old boy just fired the quill down on the book, and roared, 'That's not an occupation. That's a bloody disease!' The first time in his life he ever swore, but his lovely manuscript was ruined. That's what registering gets you into."

"One of them Brogans was stone mad anyway," I added. "Sure one of them came to me, I don't know which one, probably number two, as you put it, for the other fellow was married in Perth. He was seeking work, as I was then looking after the digging of some stanchion holes outside Edinburgh. He told me he was after leaving hospital in Dunfermline, where he had been treated for a nervous breakdown. I admit he didn't look too solid on it, as he kept opening his mouth and wriggling his jawbone about, when talking to you. However the poor fellow had to eat, so I sent him along to John Digby who was struggling in a hole on his own.

"About twenty minutes later, Digby came galloping across the field, with the sweat lashing off him. 'Fuck you,' he said. 'What the bloody hell was that, you send over to me? A fluking lunatic.' 'What happened?' I inquired. 'Nothing yet, he just jumped down the hole and began helping me finish timbering. OK. Then when we had finished, and waiting for the ladder to be lowered, he turned and stared at me, with the muck graff in his hand. "I'm just out of the bin," said he, as he started making faces at me, and slavering at the mouth.' 'What bin,' I stammered. 'The loony bin,' he answered.

"'By cripes I didn't need any ladder to get out of that hole—cripes, man, he could have killed me with the graff. You go down into a hole five-foot square, ten-foot deep, and stand shoulder to shoulder with a man making faces at you, while telling you he has just been let loose from the loony bin, and see how you like it.'

"I had to send Brogan away on his own as nobody would work with him. He was with me for a good while, and perfectly harmless, had he kept his mouth shut he would have been alright."

"He was a bit odd right enough," agreed Tinen. "I seen him once sewing a patch on his trousers. We were in camp at the time, and he sewed it on the outside, without tucking in the ragged edges. It was a terrible-looking sight, but he thought it was a masterpiece."

"Better than Snowie McFadden," said Ryan. "Though I'll admit a bit neater than Brogan, when he burned a hole in his good trousers, he just applied a bit of boot polish to the leg underneath the hole. The trousers were black you see. Somebody said it would have been more respectable had he put a black bandage on the leg, but where on earth would you get a black bandage—he would have been right enough had the suit been white."

"Somebody must have had to tell him there was a hole there, for he was too blind to see anything. He was an albino, that's what they call them, I believe," said Mull.

"That's right, but Snowie could see right enough," I said. "You play cards with him, and you would soon find out. I'll tell you a good one about him, when he was working for Big Hughie Duffy on a building site outside Oban, Snowie was labouring on the pipe-layer.

"One day when the pipe-layer was away for a crap, along came Jock, the clerk of works, and spotting Snowie sitting on the edge of the shallow trench, rolling a cigarette, he went over to him, and cast a critical eye along the newly laid line of pipes before saying to Snowie. 'I think there's a backfall on them pipes.' 'I wouldn't know, mister,' answered Snowie. 'As I'm only the labourer.' 'Well damn it man, you can see for yourself,' said the C of W, as he jumped down in the trench and placed his little seven-inch pocket level on the barrel of a pipe.

"Snowie slipped down beside him, picked up the level, and held it across his nose. 'I believe you're bloody right,' he said, as he handed the level back to him.

"The clerk of works went away dumfounded. I believe he had a cup of strong black coffee, well laced, before he went in to see Duffy.

"Typical of Snowie," I said. "But behind it all he was a good worker when doing what he wanted to do. He was a tiptop driller, for he worked alongside me in the north, no one ever seen him leaving a coat hanger on the face."

"I remember him on this job at Preston. We were shaft sinking in preparation for the drive. It was a fairly wet patch, and the farseeing general foreman had laid a line of pipes away from the site before we commenced sinking atall. This was to take the discharge from the big Sykes pump. Him being a cost-saving kind of a fellow, didn't he have a Y-branch placed in the line, to accommodate the discharge from the little toilet. A farseeing man was he.

"However, this morning the pump started farting and chugging, as apparently there was a blockage somewhere along the line. So Big Rab MacKinnock the fitter, came out of his little shack to have a look at the problem. He went over to the pump, undid the governors, and holding the throttle lever in his hand, he opened her up, damn me man, she roared as the exhaust belched a cloud of black smoke. You could see the flexible part of the delivery pipe humping its back with the pressure, then suddenly there came an almighty bang, as the flex released from pressure flopped down flat, and the nearby prowie door came flying off its hinges, firing a white-headed object flat on his face, at our feet. It was Snowie, soaked, and smothered in toilet papers, he was like a drowned sewer rat. He scrambled to his feet, his trousers round his ankles, and still holding on to the paper he had been reading as bits dropped off into the pond formed by the trousers round his feet. We stood there dumfounded waiting for him to explode. He didn't, he just looked down at himself, then looked at us and grinned. 'She's a powerful animal that one,' he said, nodding towards the pump.

"It took all morning to clean him up, and rig him out with old spare gear that was lying about the changing hut. What happened was, the pressure in the blocked pipeline backfired through the toilet connection, and caught Snowie on the throne, studying form."

"By crikey he got a rude awakening," laughed Tinen. "I would say the speed he came out that door at would try any of the horses he was studying."

"Be as it may, the same man was nobody's fool," said Mull. "He once explained to me that the truest square you can find around is the corner of a newspaper. Would you believe that? He maintained the drums of paper loaded into the printers had to be set so exact that the margin left on the printed paper wouldn't alter. The least little error, and the print would run off the edge. He had a point."

"Strangely now, I heard that in a pub in Chancery Lane once," I said. "But I had forgotten all about it."

"I see the Bundle of Rags over there," said Ryan. "When did he start, or is he just visiting?"

"Visiting, I suppose," said Tinen. "He is mainly a cable-laying man, not for the heavy stuff. Come to think of it I have never heard of him doing anything else."

"True enough," said Ryan. "I worked with him down in Southampton, and that was a cable job, a rough clouster he is at work too, a cable trench is about his limit, good crack though. The way he dresses and carries on makes it hard for him to find any kind of digs. I think he damps down too.* We had a good laugh one morning as we piled on the back of the

---

* wets the bed

wagon, the owld gangerman was standing there counting heads, when the Bundle came galloping up, with an old suitcase tied up with string, which he slung onto the wagon, a common practice. 'Fuck this,' said the gangerman. 'There is far too much of this bailing-out going on here, it's giving us all a bad name with the locals, it will have to stop.' 'Did you ever bail-out?' asked the Bundle. 'Once maybe, when I was young.' 'Ah well,' said the Bundle. 'The hen that lays out once, will always do it again,' and he jumped on the wagon."

"I have never seen him with a decent stitch of clothes on his back," said Ryan.

"Not him," added Ginger. "You will always find him between opening hours on a Saturday, rooting about among the secondhand stalls in some market. I wouldn't be a bit surprised, but he has a pile stashed away in some post office."

"Could be," I agreed. "He don't spend that much. There was a story going about that he once fell into the canal at Chalk Farm, when sloshed. Somebody shouted, 'There is a man in the water' as Joe Murphy and a mate were passing. Joe having been in the Royal Navy during the war, jumped in, and between the pair of them, managed to skulldrag him onto the towpath.

"He was crouched there in a heap on his hands and knees, trying to vomit forty gallons of canal bilge, when this old woman, half steamed, barged through the crowd of onlookers and asked, 'What's that?' pointing to the Bundle with a Guinness bottle. 'It's the Bundle of Rags,' answered Joe. 'Then throw the fucking thing back in,' said she, giving him a kick that sent him flying back into the canal."

"It wouldn't have been a bad idea at that," murmured Ryan, as he drew on his pipe, and observed the Bundle from the back.

"John Brennan told me once," I said, "that the Bundle invited him and a mate called Dingle Bell up to his gaff for a drink, one Monday afternoon when they were all dossing. Three to five thirty is a dead time with the pubs shut, so he accepted. John reckoned he never seen a rougher dive, a siege of mice on the table, so full of sugar they could hardly get off, and nothing in the room but the bed, and a box. He had plenty hooch about the place, though. Apparently he won a few bob on the horses on the Saturday, hence the party.

"As the beer was in aluminum half-gallon tins, the only vessel he had to drink from was an old aluminum teapot. For drinking the whiskey, he grabbed a holy water fount that was on the wall, by the door, washed it out in the sink, and dried it with the corner of his jacket, before filling it and handing it to John, who reckoned the wings of the surmounting angel leaned against his forehead as he drank. A slug of life's water from the fountain of life, with a draught of beer from the spout of a teapot, it must have been some party."

"I can well believe it," said Ryan. "I heard a tale about the Dingle Bell when he took digs somewhere in Liverpool. On the first night he got caught short in the middle of the night, and didn't know where the prowie was, as it was a big house, so he did it in an old sock. When finished, he opened up the window, to dispose of it, but to get it as far away from the scene of the crime as possible, he decided to swing it round his head a few times before letting go, thus leaving a clean pavement below his window.

"Now after shutting the window, and having a good scratch before returning to the flea pit, he happened to yawn, and look up at the ceiling. Holy blazes! He had forgotten there was a hole in the toe of the sock, and there stuck to the ceiling, like the rock of Gibraltar, was the object that should by all laws of gravity, be miles away enshrouded in a sock. Them Victorian-era ceilings are mighty high, so nothing for it now, but to bail out with the cock's crow.

"It was some weeks later that he happened to see the landlord in a pub he was in, as he was a fairly decent man, and to stop any shenanigan, among everyone around, he approached him, and offered him two pounds toward painting the ceiling. 'Two pounds!' the landlord said. 'Listen whacker, I'll give you five pounds, if you just tell me how you managed it.'"

"I hope the weather is a bit better tomorrow," said Ryan, changing the subject. "As I intend paying a visit to Leeds. Just to see if there is anything doing there. I heard McDaid was working about there."

"If he is, it's out at Ferry Bridge you will find him, as they are building a new power station there," I said. "There is a bit of a tunnel going on there too."

"Aye," said Mull. "But I think McDaid is a bit over it, for that caper. It's OK if you stay with it, but long breaks is deadly in that game, and worse still in timber headings."

"I don't know," said Tinen. "Tom Doonan and the Pincher were driving a heading, and they were both in their fifties, granted there was no pressure on them, as they priced it themselves, and it was only about thirty foot long. It was through an old disused single-track railway embankment, for some local builder who was laying a sewer, and had to go through it, so the pair took it on. Now wait till I tell you what happened.

"They were at it for a week, when they met as usual in the local pub at dinnertime, and started chatting about it. 'How far in are you?' Doonan asked the Pincher. 'Six settings,' he replied. 'Well damn me, I'm on my seventh, so something is wrong. I'll check after we go back.'

"Right after dinner when Doonan got back, he grabbed his short pick, they had no air tools, swiped at the side, but it was dead solid. He then had a go at the other side, damn me but a lump of muck fell at his feet to expose the other drive only inches away. Doonan shoved his head through the hole, and looked around. He spied the Pincher up at the face, busy with a hammer and wedge, and shouted, 'Hoy.' The Pincher froze, and slowly looked round, then he passed out.

"Well damn it to hell man anybody would. Down there in the silence of the grave, with nothing but a single candle for light, and seeing a head appear out of the side of the tunnel, it would take a very steady man to keep his cool. They had obviously passed each other, but I believe things came alright in the end, as it was only taking a nine-inch pipe there was plenty room for manoeuvre."

"It always struck me as a bloody shame," said Ryan, "having to drive a four-foot-six-diameter heading just to accommodate a nine-inch pipe. Of course one needs room to work, but nevertheless it is a lot of work for nothing."

"Yup," said Mull. "That's right enough, but they are working on a gadget now that augers its way through the ground, and takes the pipe with it. I don't know how it works exactly, but it does."

"I heard of the machines right enough," said Ginger. "But I would like to see one working before I would put any trust in it."

"Well, sure anything that makes our life any easier is very welcome," I said. "We haven't advanced much over a few hundred years, when you think about it."

"Mull has," said Ginger. "I see him this morning with a brand-new plumb bob."

"Probably fell of the back of a lorry," said Ryan. "Either that or he won a lab on the horses."

"I didn't know you played the horses, Mull," I said.

"Now and again I do," said Mull. "Let me tell you a true story. I was once tramping my way from Newark-on-Trent to Leicester, when who do you think I ran into, but the tramp Malone himself, perched on a mossy milestone at the Nottingham fork off, where he was after coming from, and on his way to Newark. After having a chat, and hearing my account of what was going on about Newark, he decided to join me on the road to Leicester. I found out as we walked and talked that he was as skint as I was, just a few shillings between us.

"As we struck a little place beyond Six Mile Bottom, we spotted a cardboard notice nailed to a telegraph pole, announcing a pony racing event taking place in a field nearby. 'What do you think?' said Malone. 'Should we pay it a visit, pool our few shillings, and try our luck? What we have is not worth a fart anyway, so it's in for a penny in for a pound.'

"In my time, I have been involved in many capers with Malone, very often to my regret, so after pondering over his proposition I consented to go along with it, with misgiving. We paid our entrance bob, and joined the crowd. After pooling our resources, we had the grand sum of twelve and six, plus a spare bootlace that was among Malone's share. 'Never mind the whang,' said he, as he threw the bootlace away, 'we'll be able to buy a dozen pairs ere this day is out.'

"Well our first selection, or should I say Malone's, was last. I knew nothing about pony track racing, just aware that it was something akin to flapping tracks for dogs. Our next choice was a bit better, it was third! 'Look,' said the Malone. 'We have seven and sixpence left in the kitty, so here's where we make the kill, on that very animal over there.' He pointed out a scruffy-looking pony, with four legs as far apart as those of a kitchen table, and looked every bit as stiff. He reminded me of one of the battle-worn mules we had in Burma, and I said so. 'Never mind the looks, her name is Biddy Mulligan, and if I am any judge of horse flesh, that's a winner.' 'What price is she?' I groaned, looking forward to the pains of a long and hungry walk to Leicester. 'See for yourself, he is twenty-five to one.

With Lucky Joe over there. I know that bugger of old, and he is lucky, lucky that he is not locked up.' 'I think we should go for the favourite, Black Panther,' I said. 'He is four to one, and a better bet.' 'Nonsense,' said Malone. 'No good to us, faint hearts never won fair ladies. We go for Biddy, and eat cake instead of bread.'

"Eat grass might be more to the point, I thought. He did, at twenty-five to one, which was a terrible price in a six-pony race.

"It was a five-furlong race, fairly long for ponies I thought, but never mind they were off. The course was very muddy, and they were all bunched up as they disappeared from sight behind a clump of trees and bushes. We wouldn't see them again until they were within fifty yards of the winning post. Everybody was dead quiet as they waited to see which one would be in front on their reappearance, for nine times out of ten that was the winner. Malone was craning his long neck over the railings, looking towards the bushes, as we could hear the pounding hooves approaching. I closed my eyes, but I soon opened them again when I heard Malone's roar. I gasped, for sure as hell, there was Biddy Mulligan covered in mud, and going hell for leather for the winning post! She had done it, and I'm sure Malone grew six inches as he strode towards Lucky Joe. Just as he was collecting the winnings in his two large outstretched claws, there came a howl from the direction of the bushes. It was Black Panther's jockey staggering about on foot, and waving his whip as he rubbed his knee. He was plastered in mud from head to toe.

"'Objection to the winner,' came a shout from the loud hailer. 'Hoy! Come back with my money,' came a shout from Lucky Joe, as Malone was making a break for it, while Joe was getting down from his box. Malone just changed gear. I never thought he could shift so fast, he was doing about sixty when he passed me waving at me to get moving. He never saw the old woman with a shackle pot on the boil, and selling cups of it to the punters at a penny a time. He scattered her and the pot over the fire, as he leapt like a gazelle through the sizzling steam. Whether he scalded her to death or not, I didn't wait to see, as I was fully occupied in keeping Malone in sight. Lucky Joe with his fat belly couldn't run far, but on seeing me take off in pursuit of Malone, he must have thought I was the Good Samaritan. 'Catch him,' he shouted after me. 'Get the money of him, and I'll see you right when you get back.' Some hope.

"About half a mile along the road, I saw my quarry turn off into a side road, and I followed. Suddenly I came across an old gate stuck in a tall hedge, and with Malone leaning on it from the inside, he waved me to join him, as he was too breathless to speak.

"After lying on the grass for about ten minutes to get our wind back, we managed to sit up, and shared out the loot. 'Right mate,' said he, 'didn't I tell you Biddy would make our day. God knows what happened behind yon bushes, but I know for a fact, the jockey on Biddy is a well-known tinker, so let us get to hell out of here. I know a shortcut across the fields that will take us to Melton Mowbray. The nearest port in a storm shipmate. We are eating again.'

"Needless to say by the time we reached Leicester a few days later, we were broke once more. Never mind such is life. One thing made my day, though, for as I entered the town, who was parading in front of the bus station selling lucky white heather, but the old one I last seen damn near getting scalded at the races. Apparently white heather was less of a risk than soup."

"He was one man well worth keeping away from," said Tinen. A curse just like the weather. I wonder what it's going to do; this is our fifth wet day, and no sign of it easing off."

"The walking pelter and one of the timekeepers were there a while ago," said Young Bob. "I heard them saying the forecast was good for next week."

"Thank God for that," I said.

There was peace around the table until Tinen gave a bit of a snigger.

"What's tickling you?" asked Mulholland.

"I was thinking there of the great Malone, and the time we were working in Liverpool, during the war, and of course you couldn't get whiskey in those days, but you could in Liverpool. Irish whiskey, by the way. It was supposed to have been smuggled across. The only thing Irish about it was the bottle, pure hooch. However, Malone, accompanied by this Welshman Flash Morgan, went into the Central Bar, though they only had the latchlifter between them, but poor Morgan had to follow Malone.

"'Two pints sir,' ordered Malone, as he perched his elbow on the bar, like a man that had a hundred pounds in his pocket. When he was served, he began chatting up the landlord, and we all know the same man could chat. After a while, as the bar was fairly quiet at that time of morning, Malone asked him quietly if he had any whiskey. 'Only Irish,' the landlord said. 'OK, give me a half bottle.' The landlord rooted around below the bar, and like a conjuror he produced a half bottle of Paddy's. Malone picked it up, and put it in his inside jacket pocket, then slipped his hand into his hip pocket and froze, staring at Flash. 'I've been robbed,' he uttered. 'Cripes my wallet, my ID, and ration card were in it!' He searched every pocket, but nothing. He turned to Flash. 'Didn't I have it on my bunk before I left?' he asked. 'I think you did,' stuttered the Flash. 'That's where I left it,' said he, with a sigh of relief. 'I hope,' he added as he handed the whiskey bottle back to the landlord. 'You better have this back, governor, until we return, if atall.'

"The man took it, and placed it back under the counter, calling after them. 'Good luck, I hope you find it.' A bit further up the town, they turned onto an old bomb site, and sat down on a piece of wall. 'What in the name of blazes was all that about!' asked the mystified Flash. 'Good luck, I hope you find it,' roared Malone. 'We found it right enough. Here have a swig out of that.' He produced a half bottle from his inside pocket. 'How in the name of blazes did you do that!' asked the amazed Flash. 'Elementary, my dear friend. You see I go prepared. That bottle you observed me handing yon galoot was the same bottle we demolished last night, back in the kip, only now it is full of piss. Somebody is going to get a surprise I warrant you.' 'Jases!' said Flash. 'Never have I seen anything like it! But hold the fluken line a minute. Here, you better have the first swig boyo, somebody else could have been just as fucking smart as you!' Now you see why I was laughing."

"There were not a trick in the book but he knew," I said. "Some men can get away with it, cheek I suppose. Danny Boyce and his mate came into a pub I was in, one evening, in Camden Town. It was dead on opening time. Danny went straight to the barman. 'Look, there's three of us just finished work, and our mate is just gone round to the office to collect our money. You don't mind if we sit here until he gets back?' 'Not atall,' he was told.

"They sat for a good while as Boyce kept hopping back and forwards to the door, and muttering, 'No sign of him yet.' At last he approached the barman once more. 'I say matey, it's embarrassing sitting here waiting without a drink, could you give us two pints until he comes, he can't be long.' He got the two pints, and another two, as he kept hopping to the door. You see the barman was committed, once he served them he had to keep going or lose out. After the fourth pint he called it a day, and told them in no mealy terms to piss off, so you see if you have the neck for it, you can get away with it."

"I knew a man," said Mull, "a Glaswegian, who used to pull a fast one on barmen. He would wait until they were busy, then make his way to the counter with a pound note in his hand, and shout for two pints with two whiskies, making sure the barman saw the note. Always make it a contrary order, he told me, it keeps them calculating. Then when he got his drink he handed the barman a ten-bob note. Nine times out of ten he got change for the pound. Granted, an odd clever barman caught him out, but what of it! He was doing nothing illegal."

"There are strange characters about sure enough," said Tinen. "For instance, I saw a bloke in a pub taking bets that he would pour a glass of beer or water, from one tumbler into another, without touching the glasses or the counter. He would even stand a foot away from the counter with his hands by his sides, while doing so. He won his bet."

"That seems impossible," said Ryan.

"No," said Tinen. "After he got permission from the barman to use his sink, he filled it with water, then dipped the two pint glasses into it, and filled them both by bringing them together, lip to lip. He then lifted them very carefully and placed them on the counter. One of course was upside down on top of the other, both locked full of water.

"He then placed an empty glass on the counter, and laid two pencils across the top of it. Now very gently he sat the waterlocked pair of glasses on top o' the pencils.

"After admiring his handiwork he stepped back the required foot from the bar, and with a drinking straw in his mouth he started blowing at the joint between the two glasses, but not touching them. Upon my soul! Didn't the water from the upturned glass start running down the side of the lower glass, into the supporting one, until it was empty, and the lower one full.

"Simple hydraulics, he maintained. As air is lighter than water, when forced between the two glasses, it rises inside the upturned tumbler expanding the air pocket at the top, thus allowing the heavier water to run out the joint. Clever."

"By dad, I would like to see that," I said. "It takes a bit of setting up, but well worth it, though you would need a couple of gangermen around, for the pencils."

"You would need two of those pencils the timekeepers use," said Mull. "Them with the corners on them; gangermen's pencils would be no good, too round like themselves."

"The pencil though is a handy yoke in more ways than one," said Tinen. "As far as Hamish Hamilton was concerned. You see, Hamish was browbeaten by the charger of a wife he had, so he told some of the lads who were teasing him for not going for a pint, that he dare not open his paypoke before handing it to her. It was then he was shown the pencil trick. I think it was the Long Dogherty who showed him how. At that time them paypokes with the cutaway corner were in use. It allowed you to count your notes before opening it. Dogherty showed him how to shove the pencil into the poke, pick up the corner of a note, and roll it round and round the pencil, then pulled it out. Simple. Some timekeepers were caught out by that trick, as men handed back their unopened pokes, complaining about being short. They could do very little about it. Mind you, that type of poke soon died a natural death. I often wondered how Hamish argued away the missing note, if ever. She could rant and rave as much as she liked but could do nothing once she had opened the poke."

"By God, if anybody knew how to thieve, it would have to be the Long fellow," I said. "He would steal the milk off your tea while you watched him."

"He stole that many hens from this Scottish farmer he worked for, without being caught, that the farmer maintained the Thief of Bagdad was an innocent man," added Ryan.

"Anything he saw he nicked, if it was not tied down," said Tinen. "They say he was passing a building site one night, and when he could find nothing to steal, he took a hod. Now in the name of heaven who would steal a hod."

"He stole more than that," said Mull. "He stole one of them jumping jack rammers you use for compacting the backfill in a trench, and sold it to a subbie in a Cricklewood pub. He had a partner in that venture, as it was too heavy for one. After the sale, the subbie told them to fetch it up to his place on the following evening, and that his wife would pay them, as he would be away on business.

"This subbie lived in a flat, over a secondhand shop on the High Street. So the pair landed up at her door with the monster. They offered to leave it in the lobby, so he could do what he liked with it, when he got home.

"Ah be japers! She would have none of that. She made them take it into the living room so she could see it, and not satisfied with that, she wanted to see it working, for she was not going to get a thick ear for buying a pig in a poke. Holy hell man! Can you just imagine it, hopping a jumping jack with about a ton of a thump, on a timber floor, and upstairs at that! Well now, they did it. A half dozen pressdowns on the handle, and away she went, in more ways than one. The bloody pair of them, the jumping jack, and the wife, all landed in the basement two floors below, in a cloud of stour, lime plaster, timbers, and furniture, not to mention a rake of needles, medals, pisspots, and the inevitable anchor from the shop. They got off with bruises, but as she landed on top of them, she was all right, by good luck the shop downstairs was closed at the time otherwise they would have taken the old miser with them, and perhaps a customer or two. How the subbie got out of it regarding the owners of the building we will never know, but wasn't it a damnable trick to pull."

"Be japers I heard about it at the time," said Ryan. "I was also told how they got it there, they hopped it all the way from Kilburn along the gutter, about half a mile away. Isn't it a wonder some copper didn't stop them and inquire about a missing trench! It would be good to see the pair looking around for a hole to backfill, like a thirsty horse looking for a water hole in the Sahara."

"Cripes! What an animal to steal," I said. "Of all things a bloody jumping jack, sure they could have stolen a barrow to carry it in, when they were at it."

"Too easy," said Mull. "Though I saw him with my own two eyes steal a pound note off a farmer once, as easy as light. It was on a market day in a little Scottish town, as we were having a drink. The Dogherty was not in our company but was standing by, when this farmer received a pound note from another bloke, and shoved it into his waistcoat pocket, leaving the corner visible. This to Dogherty was like a red rag to a bull, and he made for him without delay. Apparently he knew the farmer, for they got chatting right away. I was unaware of the pound's existence until Dogherty started tapping the farmer on the chest with his crooked forefinger, in a good-natured way.

At first I thought it was the heavy gold watch chain he was after, but on realising it was heavy enough to anchor the *Queen Mary*. I looked further. It was then I observed the pound note, which seemed to have a life of its own, for every time Dogherty tapped the waistcoat it seemed to rise a bit further in the pocket. Finally on the last tap it disappeared completely, into Dogherty's fist, and that was that. As easy as you like."

"Good luck to him," I said. "The farmer would not go hungry for the want of a pound, but he would miss it just the same."

"You know something," said Mull. "It is surprising the number of navvies who spent some of the war years among the farmers, dodging the column of course, but most of them were eventually caught out, and had to do their stint. Surprising too are the number of conscripts that are honest enough to own up, and say they were conscripted—only navvies, Glaswegians, and the Cockney barrow boys will admit it. When I did my stint, the only regulars I met were the instructors here in Blighty, and as for volunteers, you could count the number I met on one hand, among the umpteen thousands of men I served with. Everyone I knew were all eagerly waiting for their demob number to come up, yet nowadays wherever you go, be it service clubs or pubs, it is all, 'when I joined up'. I have yet to hear 'when I was conscripted.' Well, all I have to say to those hypocrites, it must have been the millions of conscripts that did all the fighting, and dying, for none seems to have come home.

"When talking about farmers," said Tinen, changing the subject away from war, "the Glutton Logue was the boy for them, as you know he had a terrible reputation for eating anything that didn't talk back to him, as he said himself. I heard he went to see this farmer, somewhere up around the border area, and asked him about temporary work. It was wartime, and wintertime, so needs must when the devil drives, as they say—building work was out at the time. The farmer said he was indeed looking for a hand, for a few months, but as his bothy had been burned down by the last culprit who stayed there, he would have to 'live in'. That meant grubbing and sleeping in the farmhouse. The Glutton didn't like that, but said he would accept. 'Weel,' said the farmer, 'as ye ken things are guy tight the noo, so ah would like fine te ken what ye would like te eat fer breakfast and such?' 'Ach,' said the Glutton. 'A good bowl of porridge, and three or four slices of bacon with two eggs will do rightly. Plenty tay and bread, though.' 'Ah see,' said the farmer, "noo for yer dinner?' 'Oh, you forgot the elevenses. For that I'll have some bread and cheese, but for the dinner, a lump of roast with plenty vegetables and potatoes will do nicely, I like a lot of potatoes, about a dozen or two. Then a good pudding to fill any holes left over. Oh, I forgot the soup, the thicker the better, and don't worry about the evening meal, for something like the dinner will do nicely.'

"'Weel, weel,' sighed the farmer, 'ah doubt ah canna afford ta take ye on laddie, but dinna be doon hearted, for ma friend across the way is looking for a chiel, for a few months. I ken fine he is desperat, so gang and see him, but afore ye gang awa, if he does start ye, ah will gie ye an extra pound a week if, when ye need a crap, ye come and do it on ma land.'"

"By what he intended to eat, he would be worth his weight in gold for that," laughed Ginger.

"I saw him eat two boiled goose eggs at one sitting," I said. "Some farmer's wife gave them to him, or so he said, perhaps he stole a page out of Dogherty's book."

"He was a huge man, though," said Ryan, "and a mighty powerful one at that. He was one night at a travelling fair in Dundee, where there was a boxing booth among the side shows. Well you know the score, it was also a wrestling booth. Parading on the stage in front of the tent were a pack of 'come all ye' hounddogs, boxers, and wrestlers. Had you put a rake on hell you wouldn't get worse looking, for there wasn't a nose nor an ear among the dollop of them. The proprietor was shouting out the terms on offer to anyone willing to commit suicide in the ring with any of them. As the Glutton and a little mate called McClusky joined the crowd of onlookers, the terms for lasting three minutes in the ring with a manmountain of a wrestler, was given as a pound a minute.

"'Fuck him. I'd eat him for breakfast,' muttered the Glutton aside to his mate, but some onlookers heard him, and the clamour started, persuading him to challenge, and he bloody did too.

"This was all the bold proprietor wanted, for now there was a surge to get in, to witness the maiming of the Glutton by this gorilla who called himself the Ghoul. I'll admit he looked the part. However the brave Glutton stripped off to his waist, and handed his clothes to McClusky, acting as his second. Then tucking his trousers into his socks, he climbed into the arena, that both his big toes were sticking out through his socks was elementary.

"Big as the Ghoul looked when pouncing about on the stage outside, he had nothing on the Glutton, when side by side in the ring. They shook hands and dived for each other's throats, or so it looked. The wrestler was a trained man, but the Glutton was tough, having spent a lifetime shovelling muck. You could see the wrestler was aware of this, and kept manoeuvring to get some sort of a grip on him that would put an end to his few moments of fame in the big lights, but the Glutton was having none of that, and made himself as awkward as possible, which wasn't hard. At last they fell in a heap on the floor, and the Ghoul got him by some kind of grip within the tangle of arms and legs, and this brought a mighty yelp from the Glutton. Now a yelp is a yelp by standards, but a yelp from the Glutton was an almighty roar. He untangled himself faster than a kitten would from a ravel of wool, and with a bear's growl he grabbed the Ghoul by what little hair he had and the left ankle, and waltzed him round in a complete circle, and with a mighty screech, sent him off into orbit. He made a touchdown about six rows of seats back, among the spectators. Not content with that, the Glutton climbed over the ropes, and the front seats, trying to get to him, to inflict more damages, but the broken-up Ghoul was off as fast as he was able, lunging for the door, more like the Hunchback of Notre Dame that the boastful braggart that pranced around on the outside stage a few minutes earlier.

"The Glutton got fully paid, no one knows how much, but they wanted rid of him fast, and he was told not to come back, methinks neither did the Ghoul."

"He was at the Barrows in Glasgow one Sunday morning," said Mull, "that was the Petticoat Lane of Glasgow, where you could buy anything, and witness all types of hoop men and conjurors at work. There was a powerful-built Dublin man there regularly, who challenged anyone to tie him up with this rope he had, that was thick enough for a tug-o'-war team. He would also lie down with a dirty big stone on his chest, and asked you to break it with a fourteen-pound hammer. This Sunday the Glutton stepped in, and drew such a wallop on the stone, he damn near embedded it in the man's chest, somebody said he was never seen there again."

"Probably going about Argyle Street with a hump on his back singing for his supper," said Ryan. "An appropriate hymn for him to sing would be 'Rock of Ages'. A second Mea Culpa."

"Bugger off the pair of you," I said. "I knew that lad well. Sure that was only a sideline. Didn't he work as a hod carrier for Charlie Kelly. I'm sure he was the answer to every brickie's prayers, as far as lintels were concerned. For his height, he was a well-built man, and a fitness fanatic. A very nice bloke to. True enough the Glutton did break that stone on his chest, but it didn't take a move out of him, he was a tough one."

"A terrible job that hod-carrying," said Tinen. "How anybody stick it I will never know, yet some men would do nothing else. A brickie was telling me about a young fellow sent on the hod by this ganger, just for a day as the right carrier was missing. After watching him perform for a wee while, the ganger approached him, and told him to get a move on, also telling him he had the hod on the wrong shoulder. 'I know,' said the young fellow, 'it should be on your shoulder.' Smart young fellows going about nowadays."

"Smarter than the gangerman anyway," said Tinen. He was no jack-hammer."

"That reminds me," I said, "about a bloke who was working on this cable trench in North London, and using a jackhammer. Whatever messing he was at, didn't he put the point of the hammer right through his wellie. He should have been wearing boots for that caper. Anyway he was lying there moaning as the rest gathered around him, dithering about what to, and were in the act of pulling the jackhammer off him when the brains arrived on the scene, the gangerman. 'Do you want him to bleed to death?' he shouted, as he made them cart him away to the North London Hospital, on a makeshift stretcher.

"On arriving there, the casualty nurse, who happened to be a man, looked at his patient, stretched out on the floor, with a fluking big jack-hammer lying on his chest, and remarked as cool as you like: 'When is the compressor coming?' He must have been around."

"Why the bloody hell didn't they unclip the point," asked somebody.

"Tut-tut," said Mull. "Too simple."

There was a bit of commotion going on at the bar. Somebody threw a rap at somebody else, and now there were a half dozen involved. We watched from our corner as they sorted themselves out. Two burly barmen were about to chuck somebody out the door, when one of his mate flattened one of them. I could see the governor on the phone. The law would be on their way no doubt. When they did arrive, they were too late, as usual, for the culprits were gone, and order had been restored once more. Just to show it somebody was singing "With My Navvy Boots On".

"What was that rumpus in aid of," asked Tinen, "or who were they?"

"No idea," I said. "But there is no harm done, just a ripple in a mill pond. There are few fighting men around today. Not like it used to be. There were hard men about those camps, but then you had to fight there, or pull freight. One of the hardest characters I ever met was a man called Devlin, a big man too. Jack Sampie and I were in this bar one Monday morning, as we hadn't faced the music, when in came Devlin, and asked the young barmaid for a pint. He nodded to us, as we knew he was barred in the same house. He was just taking his first slug, when the governor appeared in the saloon doorway. 'Got out,' he shouted at Devlin. 'You won't put me out.' 'Won't I now! Maybe not personally, but this boy will. Jim, go get him!' he shouted to a huge bullmastiff dog that was lurking behind him.

"The dog made a dive at Devlin, barking and snarling. Devlin just dropped down on his hands and knees, and started barking and snarling back at the dog. Damn me, but the dog stopped dead in his tracks, with a look of astonishment in his eyes, as he stared at Devlin. Not being sure what to do in such an unusual predicament, he just turned his head to the side, presumably to get a different slant at the object confronting him. That was his downfall, for with one snap, Devlin had him by the ear, with his teeth. The dog let out such a howl, you would think the banshee was about. When Devlin let go, the dog cleared the counter, scattering the landlord on the floor, as he was trying to make a phone call. Devlin beat it, but not before finishing his pint, and giving us a wink."

"He was obviously of the tinker stock, to do a trick like that," said Mull. "They know dogs, and their ways. Devlin knew what he was about, for it takes a brave man to tackle a bullmastiff."

"Oh, I don't know," said Ryan. "I seen Ownie Coll strangle an Alsatian, mind you it was the landlord's fault, for the dog should not have been where it was, and it attacked Ownie, so he was within his rights to defend himself."

"There goes that bell again," said Mull. "Cripes, we are plagued by bells and whistles, worse than a pack of sheepdogs. I'm getting fed up

146

with this civil engineering crack, and seriously thinking of putting my shovel away for good, too old for this gallivanting about the country. There's a townie of mine who has a little building firm in Newcastle, and he has asked me more than once if I would come and look after the yard for him, as he only employs about twenty men, with two machines, it would be a doddle."

"If I was you, I'd jump at it," I said. "As Tom Tinen here is thinking of retiring back to Ireland shortly, I'm thinking of doing something similar. The point is finding it. However, we have to go as the shop is shut, so all the best to everyone. If Monday is wet again, I might pull freight, as this job is finished anyway."

Chapter 7

The rain couldn't have come at a better time, and cheers greeted it so. In spite of the dour sky, with a forecast to match, the powers that be decided to concrete, a stupid decision on a morning that had every indication of being wet even before we started. It must have been a desperate decision after a full week of rain. We all knew the rain was coming, and now it was here, and we were in the pub, and to hell with their concrete.

"That general foreman is the stupidest man I ever snapped," said Ryan. "Instead of having us directed in some useful direction, he wanted us to concentrate on concreting that bloody bay against all odds. Now he is left with a split bay that will require an expansion joint, and we all know how architects love that."

"Don't blame the GF," said Tinen. "Directors pressure on him and the agent for production, the progress chart is dropping dangerously through adverse weather. Granted they are insured against bad weather, but that only covers costs, not profit. It's that old clouster of a concrete ganger that's to blame, for saying it could be done."

"Did you see the effects the concrete had on him once we started?" said Ginger. "A reasonable individual normally until concrete comes over the horizon, then insanity takes hold, and he is as thick as the concrete."

"How any woman can tell how her children will turn out," said Mull, getting seated, after telling a drunken clouster at the bar to go and lie down, a waster of a man who was perpetually drunk. "That clouster up there and yon gangerman are both the outcome of some mother's mismanagement."

"It is hard when there's a houseful of them," said Ryan. "I know for there were a crowd of us. Cripes when I was young, I always knew when another one was on the way, like a weather sign the owld one would appear with a card of safety pins, and a new spool of white thread, then get tore into an old flannelette sheet, tearing it into squares, that were later trimmed and edged. I knew what the damn square and pin were for, a type of catch-pit, but I was a grown man before I found out what the spool of thread was for. Now I'm wondering, in cases like yon fellow at the bar, the concrete ganger, and a few others, wouldn't it have been put to better use if tied around the neck instead of the navel."

"Yes," I said. "The safety pins were the stock in trade of the midwives who did most of the work in those days, and none of them with any certificates atall, that is, if one considers a bit of paper a licence to do what you want. They had all the practical qualifications in the world, having brought dozens of whelps into it. The local doctors knew it too."

"Considering those days, and the treatment dished out, it's a wonder we have any kind of brains left atall," said Ryan. "As soon as you were born you were dumped into a cradle, where they strived to rock the brains out of you. If they hadn't time to do it themself, it was given to some older member of the tribe, whose main aim was to knock you out as fast as possible, so that he or she could go back out to play. When you made an effort to walk, they stuck you into an old tea chest, and imprisoned you. The only good thing to come out of that confinement were the best of teeth, as you had a good frame of timber round the top, to cut them on. Danny O'Reilly reckoned that Cross-Eyed Daly suffered the most through it, him being too small to look over the top he had to look out through yon inspection hole in the side of the chest, hence the kink in the eye. Once you got too big for the tea chest, and went toddling, if you went near the door atall, they frightened the life out of you with ghost stories. A mark that stayed with some people all their lives."

"If I know anything," said Tinen, "and the Cross-Eyed's mother was as thick as himself, she would have the inspection hole up against the wall, into the bargain, and small wonder he is boss-eyed. But talking about ghosts, there was a haunted house outside a village called Barton-upon-Humber, in Lincolnshire, when we were there. All the locals believed it to be so, even one local publican had on offer a pound note for anyone who would spend a night there. Well there was one character among a bunch of boys who were laying cables in the locality, and using the pub, who decided he would have a go at the staying—a pound was a pound.

"One night after the pub closed, or at least after the doors were closed, they fixed him up with a blanket and a candle, saw him settled down in an upstairs room in the haunted house, and wished him good night, before returning to the pub, via the back door. Everybody agreeing that he was braver than them. At about half twelve the company was shattered by a hammering on the back door. It was our man, and he was in a terrible state. His clothes were thrown on, his pullover was back to front, his boots were untied, and were on the wrong feet, his two eyes were like saucers, and whatever little hair he had was sticking straight up in the air. All this I was told by a man who was there. What happened he said, as our man blew out the candle and tried to settle down to sleep, he couldn't, the whole house was moaning and groaning though there was no wind. In spite of his nervousness he stuck it out until he heard it: 'Ohhhh … whoooo … there's nobody here but you and I.' Then deadly silence. Again: 'Whoooo … there's nobody here but you and I.' That was it. Our man was half dressed in a jiffy, in whatever clothes he could get hold of, and desperately searching for his boots when, 'Whoooo … there's nobody here—' 'Fuck off!' roared our man. 'When I get my bloody boots there will be nobody here but yourself!' and he beat it as fast as his legs would carry him, back to the pub. It took about three brandies to pacify him. The teller believed the landlord was behind it all, more than likely one of his cronies did the moaning, his pound was safe, and he had another story to tell."

"Easy enough done," I agreed. "Sure the man was primed before he ever went near the place. In the old days back in Ireland, when some old local died, all you heard at the nighttime wake were ghost stories. You were frightened to death of going home alone, therefore you stayed till daybreak. There were methods in their madness, as it kept company about during the long night."

"All hypocrites," said Ryan. "Ghosts and phantoms are anti-religion. Ministers and priests are not believers of ghosts, so why should anybody else be. Personally I think, when you go down you stay down. Maybe some people were put down while still alive in past times, mistaken for dead, but not in Ireland, by no means. There they sit watching you for three days, and nights, to make sure you're dead, and not being content with that, they make a ceilidh of it, with rakes of booze, and food around, so anybody that don't stir after three days of that is definitely dead. If not, he ought to be."

"I remember when working with McAlpine once, a man got killed on site," said Mull. "So we were all given the day off to go to the funeral. It was a big do. There were six of his cronies under the coffin, as he was a big man, and his gangerman was in charge of the firing party, as you might say. When they got to the bier in front of the altar, and the priest who was leading them turned round to face them, he noticed something adrift, so he whispered to the gangerman, 'Reverse the coffin.' The old ganger just stared at him, scratching his ear, and shuffling his feet. 'Reverse the coffin,' the priest repeated, slightly louder, and slightly agitated. Then seeing the gangerman's confusion, he made a little circular gesture with his finger. 'Oh ho!' said the ganger, giving a little jump, and glowing with comprehension. 'Right lads, slew the fucker round.' It was done."

"They would understand that," chuckled Tinen. "When I was a boy, I heard them telling about some old man that was dying—he was well over ninety when he became ill. Those were the days when the main bed was in the living room, and it was on this bed he was lying in his sickness, with the neighbours calling in to see him, and to wish him well.

"A long string of a fellow, called Roary More, because of his height, went to see him one day. Roary was a big awkward man. 'How are you,' he asked, as he stood in the middle of the floor, kneading his cap. 'Ach. Only fair to middlin,' came the weak reply. 'Ach! Hell man,' said Roary, 'you'll live awhile yet. Tis only a slight drawback, you will be just as right as rain after a few days loafing in the bed.' 'Will you have a cup of tea, Roary?' asked one of the fussing granddaughters. 'Not atall Mrs Woman, sure I'm just after wiping me mouth,' said Roary. It was a saying of his.

"However he stayed for a little while before saying cheerio to the bedridden man, then with a further 'I'll be seeing you,' he made for the door, with the hurry that was on him, and talking to those behind him, didn't he forget the low door. His memory was soon jogged by the crack of his head against the stone lintel. It nearly split him open. 'Holy jases, woman!' he shouted. 'There's no four fluking men will get a coffin out that bloody door!' The owld fellow on the bed couldn't help but hear him, and proved him very wrong, for they did carry him out a few days later."

"Very diplomatic people," said Ryan, "but sure they took a rather casual look at death, providing it didn't come sudden, or to the young. Neighbours did all the necessities, the washing and laying out of the corpse, dug the grave, and backfilled it too. In fact I heard of a man that lost his ailing wife one morning, and while the local women were doing the business, he went to the local store, for the shroud. There he was heard arguing with the shopkeeper about the price of it, saying to him, 'Heavens man! That's robbery, too dear altogether.' So he went further afield.

"On his return journey the first shopkeeper was at his door as he passed, and asked him where did he get the shroud, and how much did he pay for it. Not believing what he was told, he asked if he could have a peep at it. So our man tore a wee corner of the parcel for him to feel it. He did. Then with a shake of the head he muttered, 'Ach, no good, she will have her knees out through it in a week.'"

"A Pole who worked along with us on a rock tunnel once was telling us about his young days in the coal mines back home," I said. "We all know that when a man gets killed in a mine, everybody goes home for the rest of the shift. In his time back in Poland, when this happened, they used to hide the body behind some shoring or such, until the end of the shift. Then declare it. Hard days."

"Aye times were hard," said Ginger. "A comical story told me by a Geordie once, up around the north. It concerned a family, I think he said there were about nine of them in it, there were six of them going to school anyway. The youngest of the school lot was always late, so the master cornered him one day and asked, 'John, how come you are always late for school, and the rest are not?' 'I have to wait my turn for the spoon, haven't I?' he replied."

"Hell's bells," laughed Mull. "That's worse than the two old ones who were having dinner—he was wolfing away good style, but she was just sitting there looking at him. When asked the reason why, she answered, 'I'm waiting for the teeth.' Now then!"

"Ah bugger off, the pair of you," said Tinen. "Seeing we are on about food, I happened to meet Jack Sampie one Monday morning while in Portsmouth as we were heading in the same direction, the pub. He was in fine fettle, for a Monday, but like myself, he didn't face the music that morning. We were strolling along, nice and quiet like, chatting away as there were a few minutes to wait before latchlifting time. As we were passing a little butcher's shop, Jack said, 'Hold on a minute I have something to say to this man.' He was Jack's butcher, as he lived nearby. 'Morning Paddy,' said the butcher, with a grin. 'Nice one.' 'Morning,' answered Jack. 'A bit nicer than that steak you sold me on Saturday.' 'Why! What was wrong with it?' 'Nothing much, except that you would die of the hunger chewing the bloody stuff.' The butcher enjoyed that so much, he told Jack to call on his way back, for another bit."

"Jack had an answer for everyone," I added. "We were rained off once, and in the Yorkshire Grey, in Portsmouth, just the pair of us, as the rest of the gang were somewhere else. They did a mighty fine dinner in the Grey, and that was before every Tom, Dick, and Harry were at the pub cooking. I noticed an old clouster of a gangerman, from a neighbouring site, wolfing into a mighty plateful, at a corner table. He must have had a standing order, for his plate was loaded. I remarked to Jack about the amount on his plate. Jack glanced over his shoulder towards him. 'Ach,' said he, with disgust. 'That man has the famine still on his mind.'

"Jack was no great believer in big feeds, little and often, he always maintained, but what he did eat was good. When you mentioned food to him, he would tell you it was only a habit, he wouldn't agree that the drink, or hooch, as he called it, was a habit."

"Habit or not, you won't go far without it," said Mull.

"It's strange," said Ginger, "that a lazy man eats more than an active man. Perhaps he has more time as he has nothing else to do."

"I think the laziest man I ever met was a man who lived near us at home," said Ryan. "Whether he was a big eater or not I don't know, but I do know he was bone idle. Going back a while in years and the springtimes, when all the little fields had to be delved, most people bought new spades—that's if the old one was done. You all know that a new spade needs sharpening before it's any good in tough ground. Well this character had bought himself a new one in the nearby town, about three miles away, and to avoid the job of sharpening, he tied the handle of it to the bicycle carrier. Thus leaving the implement to trail behind, so that the road surface would do the job for him—wasn't he the brainy bugger.

"It's true that if you want to find the easiest way of doing anything, give it to the laziest man on site to do and he will find it. However, our man coming along the road met with a local man going the other way, so they stopped for a crack, and of course the new spade came under scrutiny. 'What do you think of it?' asked our man. 'Well,' said the neighbour. 'It's going to a good home anyway.' There weren't going to be much abuse there."

"Shovels or spades need looking after like any other tool," said Mull. "A good clean shovel makes life a lot easier. Damn me man, and I'm speaking for all of us, how often did we make a fry-up, on the shovel. Cleaner than any frying pan, and why wouldn't it be. Good Sheffield steel, burnished in clean hard ballast, either behind the mixer or in the true earth. Look at the shovels used by today's clowns, half a hunder-weight of muck and cement stuck to it. Haven't the intelligence to clean it off. When did you last see a man grabbing a handful of grass and go to the nearest puddle to clean his shovel, before putting it away, no time for that, but all the time in the world to stand up to roll a cigarette. Every three shovelfuls they lift could be done in two with a clean shovel, but then they reckon to be smarter than us nowadays. Did you ever notice how natural it appeared, when every man went to the toolbox in the morning and just picked out his own shovel, you would swear it had his name on it? You always knew your own shovel by the feel of it."

"Strange," said Tinen, "how they never use the square-nose shovel in Scotland, always the Bulldog shovel, granted they are a bit heavier than the square nose, but the point is great for digging. Damn near as good as a pick."

"Heavy, but you get used to them," said Ryan. "In Ireland they use the long shovel, yon handle must be about eight feet long. I suppose it's to keep them well away from work."

"More for using as a chin rest," said Mull. "I suppose it is easier on the back, as you take the strain on the knees. You don't do the bending you do with the short shovel. I would find it a bit difficult without the hand grip, but I would say it must be a great tool for loading a high wagon."

"Oh, that's what they were made for, shovelling loose material," said Tinen. "Sure no shovel was made for digging—if it were, there would be a footrest or lug on it, just like a spade. So we make our own footrest, or foot iron, as it's called, to fix on the instep of our boot, thus allowing us to dig with the shovel."

"The most awful implement ever invented by man," said Ryan. "The galoot that invented it should be permanently shod with five of them. One on each foot, one on each hand, just like a horse, and the other shoved up his arse for luck. Believe me or not, I have seen a man down in a stanchion hole digging like hell in his bare feet, with the foot iron, tied to the bare instep. Granted it was summer, and the hole was very wet, in fact the water would be over his boots, had he kept them on, the dig was also soft clay, but how the hell could you make excuses for an animal like that. There was some comfort in the fact that the hole was well away from public gaze, in the middle of a meadow full of grazing cattle, and one donkey, down in the hole."

"You don't see much of the foot iron nowadays," said Tinen. "Nor do you see the yorks either."

"Now that was a great practice, the yorks," I said. "Man they were handy for keeping the weight of the moleskins off your back. Of course they were known by various names, depending on the locality you were in. Some people called them just plain kneestraps. The main point was their common use, irrespective of name. Not only did they keep your back easy, but they kept your trouser bottoms dry, if there was any water about. Wearing the yorks gave you bags of room around the knees too, especially when working in confined spaces, like tunnels or headings. Do you realise the gentry copied the idea for their plus fours, which they wear when golfing or shooting, bags of room around the arse, and knees. Of course they gave them a high-sounding name, and used stockings to cover up the garters. Later on they tailored the trousers to just below the knee, and discarded the garter or yorks in favour of buttons sewn on the trousers, another type were the knee breeches."

"Ach, but sure the Spaniards were wearing pantaloons long before yorks were ever thought of," said Mull, "but then there were navvies before the Spaniards, back in the Roman times. Who else built them aqueducts that are still standing today. Of course they didn't call them navvies then—they were called by their proper name, slaves. Names do little to conditions methinks."

"Slaves! Huh, some slave you," said Ryan. "When you go to that pigeon hole on Friday, and the timekeeper tells you there's fuck all for you, will soon show us whither you are a slave or not. Though a bit of the lash across the haunches would do nothing but improve your movements."

"I'm in complete agreement," said Tinen.

"A bit of slavery would do him no harm atall," said Ginger. "It might take away that beer gut he has for starters. Let us face it, timbering is a lazy man's job, but admittedly an essential one, on big sites, though I have yet to see any of them slaving."

"There are still plenty of slaves being used in the world today," I said. "Especially in the Far East and south seas. You go to India or any of those Chinese ports, and you will see them loading coal on ships, not to mention doing other kinds of work. Their bosses get round the lag by maintaining they look after their welfare, by paying them a meagre wage, with clothing, and food thrown in, then call them coolies. Those rich Middle Easterners have slaves to attend on their womenfolk, or harem."

"Ah, but they are dressed," said Mull, "just the same as a tomcat, so they can do no damage to the women. It is said they make great singers."

"You would sing too, if you got the same done to you," said Ryan.

"Beats me why they want a siege of women for anyway," said Tinen. "One hairpin is enough for any man, but them desert people are hard— they have to be to stick the conditions there."

"A Cockney was telling me once about the desert. He was out there with the Montgomery lot, chasing Germans, all over the place," said Mull. "He said there was a pair of Irishmen along with him, who buggered off into the desert. In other words they went on the run. 'Damn me, mite,' he said. You know how them Cockneys speak. 'They were out there for bleeding weeks, just going round in circles. All they had was some water, some hardtack, and their rifles. They were bleeding lost, matey. Then one day they sees this Arab geezer coming along, sitting on a camel, and all dolled up in rags, but all them desert Arab geezers look that way. One of the lads cocked his rifle, and aimed it at the Arab. 'Get dahn of that bleeding camel, and tell us where we are,' he demanded. The hairy-faced geezer on the camel just stared at them for a while, then says, 'Begorra, put dahn that gun. I've been out here since the bleeding Fourteen War.'"

"One of ours again," said Tinen. "Fair play to him, he managed to get hold of a camel anyway. Paddy Quinn spent a long time among them, with some contractor. He said they were all right to work with, a bit excitable when things went wrong, but otherwise OK."

"Long time since Paddy and I were in digs together," I said. "It was in the southside of Glasgow, a place called Cumberland Street. Full of lodgers, as every house took them in, as an additional source of income. Some of those landladies kept the Barrowland 'cat and dog scraps' stalls in business.

"We were staying on the second floor in a tenement block. Four of us sharing the one big room, in two double beds. Quinn and I shared one bed, and a young fellow whose name evades me shared with a cantankerous old bugger. They never stopped arguing about the bedclothes, one accusing the other of hogging the lot. I know the young fellow had the best of it, as he was over against the wall, and could therefore pin the blankets to the wall, with his knees. Now every morning the landlady came into the room with a big basin of porridge, and a jug of milk, which she placed on a large round table, that stood in the middle of the floor. So when you got up, you just picked up one of the four plates that were provided, and helped yourself to the porridge.

"This Sunday morning, Quinn and I were the first up as it was getting late and the porridge was getting cold—neither of us liked it cold. The other pair were still snoring, lying cheek to cheek, as you might say. The young one, his nose and knees to the wall. The owld one, his nose and knees hanging over the front of the bed.

"'Well fluke that pair,' I said. 'They were arguing all bloody night about the bedclothes, after the young buck came in about two o'clock and wakened the other fellow. I'm sick listening to them.' Needless to say being a Sunday morning, I was in a bad mood, after the usual Saturday night's session.

"'So am I,' said Paddy, as he glanced across at the innocent-looking pair. 'But I'll fix the fluking two of them good and proper.' He got up from the table with a spoonful of porridge, and crept quietly towards to the bed. Then he eased up the bedclothes slightly, and dropped the porridge right between the sleeping pair. As the bedclothes were well down about their waists, the porridge landed well down the bed, and not one move did they make as Paddy came back to the table. We carried on eating our porridge, but as I was facing the bed I was keeping an eye on events. After a while the old boy turned on his back, with a little cough. Then as he went to pull the clothes up under his chin, his eyes opened wide, staring at the ceiling. He lay there like a corpse for a few minutes, before I saw his hand going down under the clothes, to feel around. Well damn me man, he sat up in the bed as if he was shot, then swung his other fist in a mighty arch to land on the young sleeper's jaw with a thump. It would have knocked out a bullock, but not the young boyo, for he was out of the bed in a flash, skull-dragging the owld fellow with him by the throat. Thank God, Quinn and I were dressed ready to go out, so we just put on our jackets, and slipped away quietly. I never heard how it all ended, for neither of the pair were in residence when we came back. They had bailed out lock, stock, and barrel."

"It is like a trick he would do," said Tinen, with tears running down his face. "He was a bugger, and there is no doubt about it. I know what he was like in camp, as we shared the same hut down in Wales. If he wasn't making French beds, he was up to something else. There were a lot of sheep roaming around the camp, as we were up in the hills, and he managed to fix a white helmet on a big ram once, by making two holes in it for the horns—helmets were made of felt in those days. It was funny to see the ram strutting around like a shift boss.

"The sheep around the camp were as tame as domestic goats, for the lads were forever feeding them pieces of bread, and as the huts were levelled off on stilts to compensate for the mountain slope, there were plenty room under the floors, which made a great shelter for them. In fact some of the lads reckoned they were better off than us."

"Is there any difference between Welsh sheep and Scottish sheep?" asked Mull.

"Not unless you sleep with them," chuckled Ryan.

"Piss off," said Mull. "Serious though, the Highland Scot go for the little black-faced fellow, while the lowlander prefers the white-faced cheviot. I heard there was a different breed in Wales."

"There are I believe," I said, "but I don't know the name."

"I hope the sheep is not as contrary as the old boyos in the pubs there," said Ginger. "I spent a month there without speaking to any."

"Ach, the Welsh are no different than us," said Mull. "Proud of their history and language, and more importantly they like nothing better than a good drink and a scrap after a hard day below the ground."

We all raised our glasses and said, "I'll drink to that."

THE END

The Old Tramp Navvy's Prayer

Bury me over by yonder mound where I know there's a heavy sod.
Bury me deep in the earth that I know, far away from the wrath of god.
For I've been a navvy all of my days, I've dug the hole and the ditch.
I've helped to make the motorways, I've helped some men grow rich.
I've racked my guts to drill and muck through highland rocky veins.
To see men die with none to cry over their broken up remains.
I burned in the sun, I froze in the snow, I cursed all my kith and my kin
With nothing ahead but a dosshouse bed and the drink at some local inn.
Now that the years have taken their toll, I'll hang up my drum and my kit
And yon gangerman will raise his hand when the last red lamp is lit.
Bury me deep in the earth that I know, keep the sun from this furrowed brow
And throw away that worn pick, for I do not need it now.
Your thoughts for this man that slept by the way, be it a hedge or a ditch.
His god had forsaken this sort of a man, for he did not live as such.
You may say he had chosen the stoney way, but what option could he find
But to plough life's stream to build some men's dreams, a monument to his kind?

—*Paddy Byrne 1926-2010*